THE
AWAKENED
MIND

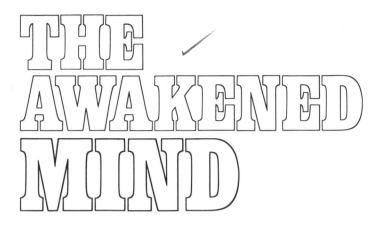

THE AWAKENED MIND

Biofeedback and the
Development of Higher
States of Awareness

C. Maxwell Cade &
Nona Coxhead

Delacorte Press / Eleanor Friede

4194330
DLC

1-18-80

reproduced 3-1-80 by

Published by
Delacorte Press/Eleanor Friede
1 Dag Hammarskjold Plaza
New York, N.Y. 10017

Manufactured in the United States of America

First printing

Designed by Laura Bernay

Library of Congress Cataloging in Publication Data

Cade, Cecil Maxwell.
  The awakened mind.

  Bibliography: p. 229
  Includes index.
  1. Biofeedback training.   2. Consciousness.
I. Coxhead, Nona, joint author.   II. Title.
BF319.5.B5C3   152.1'88   78-13078
ISBN 0-440-00244-3

ACKNOWLEDGMENTS

It is perfectly clear that with a book of this type, covering so much new ground, it is necessary to spend a good deal of time in considering the work of one's predecessors in the field.

The scope of the bibliography gives a fair indication of this kind of coverage. But although the number of individuals is too large to be mentioned, there are a few whose help must be recorded: Dr. Ann Woolley-Hart, whose aid in the early days is gratefully acknowledged; Mrs. Addie Raeburn, Mr. and Mrs. Edgar Chase, Major Bruce MacManaway, and Mrs. Rose Gladden, to whom both the authors are in vast debt; His Divinity Swami Prakashanand Saraswati, who taught the authors more than he knows; and lastly Jules Cashford and Geoff Blundell (Audio Ltd.) for reading this book in manuscript, correcting it, making innumerable suggestions.

vi ACKNOWLEDGMENTS

Our thanks to all the foregoing, and to Bridget Berry for doing some of the line drawings in the text, John C. Gowan, and Isabel Cade, without whose help this book could not have been written.

Preface

In writing this book, I am well aware that biofeedback—the voluntary control of what were heretofore considered involuntary states—is already widely known as a new and extremely promising medical tool for the control of those elusive psychosomatic and stress diseases that so beset modern society, especially in the West.

I am also aware of the highly important research being done by many notable workers in this field to extend the range and scope of benefits from instrumented self-control.

My work, however, while fully incorporating the basic biofeedback principles and techniques in all their aspects, has branched off into a singular direction and emphasis—that of combining biofeedback training and monitoring with the ancient art of meditation so as to try to achieve a maximal mind-body awareness, this in turn leading to the gradual development of higher levels of consciousness.

During several years of intensely channeled research in both lab and classroom, the latter involving some four thou-

sand students who took my courses in self-awareness training, I established the existence of a measurable hierarchy of
states of consciousness, each one a stage in a progressively
more integrated pattern of electrical activity of the brain.

Since, up to this time, all existing schemes proposing
hierarchies of states of awareness were based on purely subjective impressions of their relative positions, I subsequently
concentrated all research effort on identifying these levels
with instrumental precision and made it a major goal to establish physiological correlates of these various states. Fortunately, I was to be given invaluable help through the exper-
tise and technical skill of Geoffrey Blundell of Audio
Limited, who worked unsparingly to meet my requirements,
and as a result, provided me with instruments of increasing
sophistication, culminating in the Mind Mirror.

Extended research with this instrument, which shows up
states of consciousness in distinct patterns of light which can
be witnessed and recorded, has confirmed that the hierarchy
of levels does indeed exist, and that there are more levels in
its ascending scale still to be measured. It has also shown that
the level of consciousness in which masters of Eastern philosophies probably spend the majority of their lives has a definite measurable pattern, as does that of healers when in the
process of their particular form of healing, the pattern often
transferring itself to the machine of the one being treated.

It is mainly of this unfolding potential within man that I
write here, believing that we have reached a beginning of the
bringing together of the outer science of technology and the
inner science of the soul. I believe we are at the frontiers
of human self-knowledge, and in sharing the evidence
herein with a wider reading public, I earnestly hope it may
accelerate the day of man's higher development.

—C. MAXWELL CADE
London, 1978

Contents

ix

THREE
Biofeedback and the Healing State

It is my firm belief that the experience of higher states of consciousness is necessary for survival of the human species.

—John C. Lilly,
The Centre of the Cyclone

ONE
Biofeedback and States of Self-Awareness

Chapter 1

A New Way of Learning– Internal Cues

There are several far more comprehensive books by prominent researchers than this one sets out to be, dealing with the fundamental clinical and potential aspects of biofeedback (see Bibliography), but in order to lay the foundation for what has evolved in our particular line of research in the field, it is necessary to cover some areas of the same territory, especially for those who come new to the idea.

Essentially, biofeedback is a new way of learning about ourselves, or a way of relearning, or realizing for the first time, what the body already knows—how to act, how to feel, even how to heal—if we listen to it. With biofeedback instruments and techniques, the art of listening to internal cues can be restored, or established. Since one cannot control that of which one is unaware, biofeedback can be said to provide the means to become aware—acutely aware—of ourselves, and thereby to gain the possibility of self-control.

For we are an inseparable body-mind unity, and it is only

3

by becoming aware of our related mental and bodily functions that we recognize their unified effect on our health,
well-being and inner development. If we are to achieve dom-
ination over our individual experience and growth, then it
follows that we must develop maximum awareness of ourselves, of our own bodily and mental states.

Through electronic monitoring of biofeedback, these bodily changes can be measured and recorded as well as per-
sonally felt. The conviction that results is the doorway to a
new, expanded realm of self-control and self-unfolding.

The actual basis of the biofeedback principle is very simple: if one is enabled physically to observe in one's self some
biological happening of which one is not normally aware, for
example, the presence of what is called the alpha rhythm in
one's brain waves, then one can be trained to control that
happening. In cases of alpha rhythm, the subject may be
trained to produce at will more of the appropriate state of
calm, detached awareness with which it is associated. So one
aspect of biofeedback is the training of the individual to control his own states of awareness, just as one aspect of the
Eastern philosophies of yoga, Sufism or Zen is the training of
the individual to control his own internal awareness at will,
but without outer technical corroboration. In other words, it
might reasonably be said that biofeedback is an instrumented
mystic self-control.

The chief characteristic of the biofeedback process clas-
sifies it as a *cognitive* process; this characteristic is awareness
of the relationship between mental activity and the feedback
signal initiated by the bodily activity which is being learned.

For instance, when learning to control some item of mind-
body behavior, we must first identify the item. The feedback
signal, which may be the movement of the needle of a meter
or the change in pitch of an artificial tone, is not the item to
be learned; it is only a label to identify the correct response

once it has been elicited. As an example, we are not really interested in learning to produce alpha waves, in spite of the immense amount that has been written about them; what we *are* interested in learning is the particular calm, detached state of mind which happens to be accompanied by the alpha rhythm.

Confirmation of the identification of a feedback symbol is not complete until the signal is stopped by the ending of the behavior that produced it. Thus, if one has apparently succeeded in producing the artificial tone which is the signal from a training machine indicating that the trainee is producing alpha waves, the trainee must, to complete the identification, make sure that the tone ceases when he opens his eyes, thinks about some unrelated problem, or in some similar way causes his alpha production to cease. This ensures that the tone is not switched on by some artifact.

In other modes of learning, behavior is either directed or judged by events outside the system; that is, both the behavior to be learned and the criteria for learning it are evaluated externally. In biofeedback, successful learning depends entirely upon internal efforts of the learner; the whole learning process is internally directed.

At this point, having indicated only that machines exist that can register inner states and that they can be used for training in self-awareness and self-control, it is time to discuss the machines themselves.

The commonest biofeedback instruments encountered today are the electroencephalograph (EEG), which monitors rhythms of electrical activity originating in the brain; the electrical skin resistance meter (ESR), which gives a direct measurement of arousal (roughly speaking, how wide awake you are) through the volar surfaces (palms of the hands and soles of the feet); the electromyograph (EMG), an instrument which measures the electrical impulses associated with muscle tension; and the temperature meter, using the thermistor probe, an instrument for measuring the temperature of an area of skin for training in mentally induced changes of temperature, the actual temperature being also an index of relaxation.

Biofeedback instruments are generally available from a number of manufacturers, but we required two which we had to develop for our special requirements. We needed an electrical skin resistance meter which would give objective readings of change of skin resistance, and we also developed a multichannel EEG—the Mind Mirror—which was specially designed to show the ephemeral patterns of the electrical signals from the two hemispheres of the cortex as they are happening (technically speaking, a real-time spectrum analyzer).

Since we are measuring the body-mind unity, it is to be expected that the readings from the instruments will be complementary, that is to say, the way in which the readings relate to each other gives further valuable indications. We shall describe how we use the instruments in our work, but before doing so, we have to consider some simple physiology of the brain.

The brain has three levels corresponding to its evolutionary ancestry: (1) the brain stem from the reptilian period, (2) the limbic system at the mammalian level plus the cerebellum added to the brain stem, and (3) the higher cortex. The later levels are further subdivided into right and left hemispheres, the whole brain having certain preferred communication paths. The brain stem is linked through the limbic levels to the cortex, and there are massive communication links between the two halves of the cortex.

The usual division of function between the two halves of the brain is that the left is responsible for such operations as logical thought, time-sequential analysis, categorizing and speech, and is the dominant half wherein consciousness resides; we label this left-brain type of function. The right half is responsible for such abilities as recognizing faces, understanding maps, appreciating art and music and viewing the whole, and we call this right-brain type of function.

There is division of opinion on the accuracy of this stereotype. Our experience suggests that, of the self-selected people who attend our courses, about two-thirds are left dominant. Robert Ornstein, in *The Psychology of Consciousness* (1972), claims that 95 percent of the population is left dominant, but we believe that this is the proportion of people who have the speech center in the left hemisphere and does not necessarily indicate that this is the dominant hemisphere. A. R. Luria (*The Working Brain*, 1973) gives approximately one-third as left dominant, one-third as right, and the rest as a minor left dominant.

Whenever we talk about "left" and "right" brain in later chapters, therefore, it will not necessarily mean that the left function is physically situated in the left hemisphere, even though it is likely to be in a large proportion of people.

Many people use only the left hemisphere; the first step in self-development awakens the right, bringing to our everyday life the ability to consciously avail ourselves of the right brain contents. Further progress confers the ability to decide how we use the possibilities inherent in the left and right divisions of the cortex, this "we" and "deciding" coming from an altogether higher level within us. C. G. Jung (*Collected Works* 8) called this the Transcendent Function, and from his studies on brain-damaged patients, decided that the seat of this "higher mind" was actually in the brain stem, an area of the brain more complex and with more interconnections than any other region.

At this level of the brain, the brain stem, we find also the Reticular Activating System (RAS), an area which is enor-

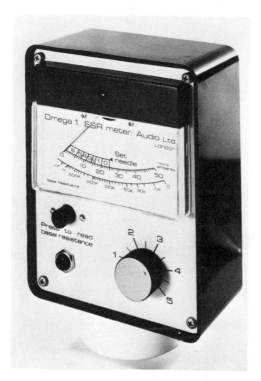

ESR METER—Electrical Skin Resistance Meter

EMG—Electromyograph

Temperature Meter

The Mind Mirror

mously important because of its role in arousal and awareness. The RAS is a functional system within the reticular formation of the brain, and is a vitally important part of the
brain stem with very widespread functions. Research on the
RAS has shown that it plays a definitive part in determining
arousal level and states of awareness. It thus has a special significance in relation to hypnosis (where attention is narrowly
directed as the hypnotist suggests) and meditation (where the
subject modifies his own attention in special ways).

Our ability to think and to perceive, even our power to
respond to stimuli with anything beyond a mere reflex, is
due to the brain cortex, but the cortex cannot function unless
it is in an aroused state—awake. The brain cortex cannot
wake itself up; what awakens the cortex from sleep and keeps
it awake is the RAS. Consciousness is impossible if the RAS
is destroyed or severely damaged.

The RAS has much wider powers than just determining
levels of wakefulness. It monitors and regulates all our muscular activity and all our sensory perceptions. Stimulating
certain areas of the RAS with an electrical current causes all
our muscular efforts to be exaggerated, as well as our sensory
perceptions, just as if the stimuli themselves had become
stronger. Stimulating other areas of the RAS causes our muscular efforts to become weaker, and our sensory perceptions,
too. It is believed that the cortex and the reticular system
operate in a feedback mode, the purpose of which is to maintain an optimum level of stimulation.

Sensations which reach the brain cortex are fed back to the
RAS, and when the level of activity becomes too high, the
RAS sends inhibitory signals to the cortex to reduce the exci-
tation. On the other hand, in a sensory-deprivation situation,
where the level of stimulation reaching the RAS via the cortex is too low, the RAS must send stimulating signals to the
cortex to maintain alertness. It is probable that anxiety states

are due to a failure of the inhibitory function of the RAS to keep cortical activity within safe limits.

It was the distinguished French psychologist M. Jouvet who first showed that it is the anterior part of the RAS which switches on the cortex during sleep to produce vivid dreams. He also showed that the posterior part of the RAS is responsible, during dreaming sleep, for inhibiting the activity of the whole spinal cord, so that the dreaming animal does not go sleepwalking and possibly endanger itself.

Most important of all, for the purpose of this book, is that the functions of the RAS provide the gateway to all forms of meditation, creative reverie and higher states of consciousness. It is cooperative action between the RAS and the cortex which makes it possible for us to achieve all the remarkable feats of self-regulation demonstrated by practitioners of biofeedback and yoga; or, to look at it another way, it is the function of biofeedback and yoga to facilitate this cooperation.

The top part of the brain stem contains the RAS, which then merges into the part of the brain termed the limbic system. The main part of the limbic system is the U-shaped hippocampus, which processes incoming information from short-term to long-term memory, and is vital to learning. At the ends of the hippocampus is the amygdala, and above is the hypothalamus. The hypothalamus and amygdala between them can generate sex drives, hunger, thirst, rage and euphoria. The limbic system seems to be responsible for many of the strange phenomena of altered states of consciousness: states of euphoria, feelings of divided consciousness (or "witnessing oneself"), loss of awareness of body boundaries, feelings of floating or flying and strange visual experiences such as sensations of white or golden light.

The RAS and the limbic system work together closely. The hypothalamus is responsible for two highly integrated responses—the fight-or-flight (sympathetic) response and the relaxation (parasympathetic) response. As we have discussed elsewhere (p. 7), the fight-or-flight response is accompanied by a *decrease* in skin resistance, while the relaxation response is accompanied by an *increase*. The peculiar Subjective Correlates of States of Arousal (p. 16) are due to the limbic-system effects mentioned above.

To return to our discussion of the machines—the main value of the *thermistor probe* is to provide an immediate feedback of the degree of control one has over one's superficial blood flow and to see instantly when one is successful or unsuccessful, and to learn, eventually, how to control skin temperature in a half-hour or so, *without* the aid of instruments. The end result is self-control learned in a very short space of time, with the added bonus of deepened conviction of the potential of the control itself.

Apart from sufferers of Reynaud's disease (insufficient circulation to the extremities, which may terminate in gangrene and the amputation of fingers and toes), thousands of people endure the misery of cold hands and feet. In training subjects by biofeedback to achieve a normal, healthy circulation, it is first necessary to break down their barrier of disbelief by proving that such control is possible.

A sensitive electrical thermocouple is taped to the subject's finger and he or she is directed as follows: "Will your finger to get hot, with all the force you can summon up." In less than a minute, the finger will be seen to have become remarkably *colder*. The forceful use of the will invokes the basic human fight-or-flight survival response and results in the diversion of blood from the skin into the muscles in preparation for violent action.

To make the fingers warmer, they must be visualized as being in a warm situation—doing the washing up, being near the fire, and so on. Temperature control has a direct relation

Cingulate gyrus

Frontal cortex

Anterior thalamus

Fornix

Hypothalamus

Pituitary body

Mid-brain

Pons

Medulla

Reticular formation

Corpus callosum

Pineal gland

Hippocampus

Cerebellum

R.A.S.

Spinal cord

to the phenomenon called *tumo*, which is the yogis' term for the power to regulate bodily heat voluntarily. In Tibet, lamas have been photographed standing in the snow for up to twenty-four hours as an act of worship or endurance.

Here is a method of self training in temperature (blood flow) control. Take the temperature probe between the thumb and forefinger or tape it to the surface of a finger, holding the extreme tip. Do not press too hard. Switch on the instrument. When you have a reading, try to increase hand temperature by *imagining* the hand in a hot situation. (If the meter reading is above 35.5°C, begin by imagining the hand in a cold situation, in order to reduce the reading.) A change of two degrees should easily be obtained at the first attempt.

After you have successfully shown increases and decreases of the temperature in both hands, place the probe in the center of the forehead and, imagining a cold pad on the forehead, reduce temperature two degrees. Successful training in increase of hand temperature and decrease in forehead temperature will often result in the control of migraine headaches.

The electromyograph, or EMG, is a device which registers and detects the voltages associated with muscle tension. Two electrodes are placed directly on each side of the muscle to be measured, and the tension voltage is fed back in microvolts (millionths of a volt), as shown by the needle or pointer on the voltage panel, or in a high-pitched sound or click, either by loudspeaker or through an earpiece worn by the user.

As a general tool for relaxation training, the EMG is of considerable importance in the development of self-awareness. Early emotional conflicts are often reflected in the body armor a person has built—permanently tense muscles intended as body defense. The electromyograph facilitates specific therapy for these states, and the ability to exercise fine control over muscular tension may be one of the best indicators of the subject's ability to relax at will, which is the gateway to meditation as well as to improved general health.

A muscle in tension or action can be recognized by the electrical activity accompanying the firing of the motor neurons. (Muscles are normally slightly tense in order to hold the body in shape and to facilitate quick responses, but should not be so tense that they are painful.) If tension is present, feedback from the electromyograph helps the subject recognize it and make an effort to reduce it with deep relaxation.

Sometimes this requires only the unlearning of a bad habit of tension, such as an almost permanently raised shoulder or a frown or a rigid neck; sometimes it is just the recognition of what mental state causes the meter to register tension that pinpoints it and leads to its elimination. EMG feedback can also dramatically eliminate the habit of subvocalization (talking to oneself under one's breath), which limits reading speed. By means of the myograph, placing electrodes on each side of the Adam's apple, subjects or students can become aware of the habit, and in a matter of two or three hours of training, can greatly increase their reading speed.

The range of uses for EMG feedback is wide. Subjects with severe facial tics have been helped, as have those suffering from insomnia, when they are taught to relax by frontalis (forehead) muscle feedback. The same method may be used in the treatment of tension headaches, because relaxation of the frontalis muscles is usually accompanied by relaxation of the neck and scalp muscles, which, when tense, produce the headaches in the first place. Anxiety symptoms are also relieved by the combination of EMG feedback and deep muscular relaxation; in fact, it is seldom that anxiety can exist in such a state of relaxation.

The electrical skin resistance meter, or ESR, consists of a

pair of electrodes typically about five centimeters square attached to the palm of each hand, a battery and a voltage meter that measures resistance of the skin to the passage of the current. Skin resistance is a mirror for all our mental and bodily states, both normal and pathological, and it can tell us very much more about ourselves than just our state of relaxation or arousal, which is why we speak of "skin talk" or the "chatterbox organ."

In the lab or classroom situation, the skin resistance is read at the commencement of the training session when subjects are in a waking state, and during the test or class, readings are taken to compare and determine the percentage difference. As the student relaxes (using various techniques shown by the instructor), the resistance increases, and the greater the relaxation, the greater the percentage of resistance change.

The device measures the number of ohms (the unit of electrical resistance) per square centimeter. Some examples are:

	ohms per sq. cm.
Panic state	50,000 (or less)
Normal state	500,000 to 1,000,000
Sleep	2,000,000 (and upward)

Arousal refers to the intensity dimension of behavior: a drowsy, inactive subject is low in arousal, while the arousal of an alert, active subject is high.

What the ESR is monitoring is the state of arousal of the subject, or the degree of activity in the sympathetic nervous system. This degree of activity varies with every response, from moods such as depression, anxiety and excitement to the intake of food and drink, drugs or smoking, the feeling of fatigue, and particularly to the time of day, since arousal usually climbs through the day and declines progressively through the night.

We have established also that a single ESR reading gives an immediate idea of what a person's hypnotic susceptibility might be, as well as detecting the possible onset of a physical indisposition. A subject with a mentally or physically lowered state of arousal will register a much higher ESR than his norm, and, conversely, a highly anxious or excited subject will register a much lower ESR than his norm. No value can be absolute for an individual, because he will register different values at each test according to the arousal of the moment. Nevertheless, it is possible to assign to an individual a characteristic resistance value for a given time of day, which (in the absence of mental disturbance or physical illness) remains more or less constant over relatively long intervals of time (months or years). Instructions we give to new students might be as follows:

"Plug in the electrode jack and attach the electrodes to the palm of the hand, so that they are sitting flat, and the elastic band is reasonably tight, but not uncomfortable. The electrodes are normally worn on the dominant hand, and in order to avoid physical movements, rest the back of the hand on the thigh or table in front of you, so that the hand and lower arm are relaxed and still.

"Press the black button on the Omega 1 ESR meter. This disconnects the right-hand control and causes the meter to indicate basal skin resistance on the bottom scale. This scale is calibrated in ohms from 10K (K = thousands) at the right-hand end of the scale to 2M (M = millions) on the left-hand end. Typical readings (when a subject is not exhausted, overanxious, very cold or apathetic) lie between the 100K and 300K indications on the scale. Note that these readings are multiplied by five to give the value per square centimeter because our electrodes have an area of five square centimeters. Wait for a few minutes for the reading to stabilize, and note that if there are large fluctuations, the subject may well be apprehensive of the meter, especially if it is the first experience. (Note: the meter is not measuring the wetness of the skin; it is possible to have a damp hand and high skin resistance.)

"Set the pointer to mid-scale—25 microamps—relax, and wait for the instructor to begin the guided imagery (see examples of guided imagery on pp. 50–51)."

Students often watch their pointers jump way up when they first sit down and may get discouraged at their apparent lack of control. They feel revealed, because until that pointer shows the fact of arousal, they may be able to hold to a façade of calmness or poise. The pointer tells the truth, too, about a depressed state or the recent ingestion of drugs or alcohol.

Sometimes on a very cold night the ESR reading will remain extremely high until the student warms up. Eventually, however, by the time the instructor starts, the pointer will have settled in the middle. From that point, as the guided imagery begins and the student follows it visually, inwardly, with eyes closed and being as relaxed as possible, the pointer should slowly swing toward a high reading, a reading that gets reliably, predictably higher as the students learn how to *feel* in order to direct it there. This visual evidence that he has direct authority over that pointer is the beginning of the student's full realization that "mind control" or mind-body unification can actually be achieved—that it is not just a theory but a demonstrable fact.

We ask students to wear their arousal-monitoring (skin resistance) electrodes all the time they are in class and to experiment with their states of arousal as much as possible by taking deep breaths, tightening muscles, relaxing, daydreaming, and so on, all of which instantly affect the reading, so that if it goes high, it must be brought down again to the middle, and vice versa. We emphasize that they cannot control that of which they are unaware; the more they can be aware of what they think or do or feel that affects their pointer, the sooner they will begin to have control over their inner states.

Use of the arousal meters is the most sensitive and accurate method known to science for showing the changes in states of arousal. We also point out that students should not confuse these meters with galvanic skin response (GSR) meters used in many laboratories to register sudden emotional changes such as shock; they are quite different, because the dynamic range of the GSR is totally inadequate for monitoring altered states of consciousness (ASC).

State of arousal varies enormously; on the meter as much as 10,000:1 between full general anesthesia and panic states. Our everyday arousal varies from about 100 to 1 between sleep and vigorous exercise. Individuals vary greatly in their ordinary levels of arousal, some are more relaxed when wide awake than others are in deep sleep. Meters are therefore calibrated both in absolute terms and in *percentage change* of skin resistance, so that they may be more versatile in use.

Most students, after the first few weeks of practice, show a normal level of arousal which varies less than 5 percent from day to day at the same time of day. Hypertense, uncontrolled individuals may show instability of zero for six or more weeks before the training becomes fully effective in stabilizing their "normal."

This objective evidence of students' or subjects' progress is extremely important to the gradual climb to higher states which the Eastern meditators have experienced for thousands of years. The principal reason we have not yet got their incredible control is that we are not self-aware to the extent that they are. Biofeedback training and monitoring gives us that awareness. In fact, a yogi, Swami Rama, who demonstrated an extraordinary range of control over his brain wave and other bodily states for Dr. Elmer Green at the Menninger Clinic in Topeka, Kansas, said that when he returned to India, he would shorten the training of novice monks by starting them off with biofeedback instruments. Many years could be saved that way, he observed.

The electroencephalograph, or EEG, is an electronic device for detecting the brain waves by means of electrodes attached to the scalp. Because the signals the electrodes pick up are very weak, the machine amplifies them and displays their strength on a meter in microvolts. The average brain wave signal reads about ten microvolts (from bi-polar pick-up).

In order to allow us to select frequencies which are of special interest, the machine has built-in filters. The signals can be visual—the swing of a needle along the range of microvolts—or auditory, a high-pitched tone. The overall procedure is too complicated for the average beginner to effectively train himself, so for the first several sessions, a trainer-operator is used who can, for example, tell the subject, "Now you're on the right note, keep going . . ."

Although the feedback signal is usually visual or auditory, it can just as well be tactile, like the vibrator which has been used to tell pilots when they are braking too hard and likely to skid. Even the use of a mirror when shaving or making up can be said to be an example of biofeedback. Perhaps the first human biofeedback instrument was our reflection in water, while the first scientific one, in the modern sense, was a mechanical arrangement of levers to fit on the head with a pointer suspended just in front of the eyes, patented at the end of the nineteenth century as a device for training people to wiggle their ears!

Before electroencephalography with all its far-reaching implications is discussed, we will briefly review the discovery of the electrical brain rhythms and the early work on brain-rhythm biofeedback.

The discovery of the electrical activity of the brain is usually attributed to Richard Caton, who, in 1875, investigated the voltages produced by the brains of monkeys and rabbits by using electrodes placed in direct contact with the exposed brain. In 1924 a similar technique was used with human beings, but it was not until later in the same year that the technique became potentially useful, when a young German scientist, Hans Berger, found that electrical signals could be picked up from the scalp without having to remove part of the skull. Berger withheld publication of his electroencephalograms for five years, but was nevertheless bitterly disappointed that his truly epoch-making work was either ridiculed or ignored for several more years.

In most individuals, one hemisphere of the brain usually shows more electrical activity than the other, but this difference tends to diminish and even to disappear when training in meditation is commenced. There is wide agreement that the alpha rhythm represents some kind of synchronous firing of neurons in the cerebral cortex.

The foundations for the biofeedback principle were laid in the late 1950s by Dr. Joe Kamiya, a psychophysiologist now at Langley Porter Neuropsychiatric Institute of the California Medical Center. The basic assumption in his alpha-control studies was that if by biofeedback a bodily event can be associated with a recognizable mental state, then it will be possible to control the bodily event.

Experiments were run in Kamiya's Chicago laboratory in which EEG electrodes were attached to the subject's scalp to register the alpha brainwave frequency. When a bell rang, the subject was to guess A if he felt alpha was present at that moment, or B if he felt it was not. He was then told at once if he was correct ("feedback").

This strangely interior form of test had surprising results. After an hour or so of haphazard guessing, the subject would begin to guess correctly up to 60 percent of the time. After three hours, some subjects became up to 80 percent correct and a few learned to guess 100 percent correctly. People could learn to "read" their own brains!

But how? When they were questioned, the subjects found they could not articulately explain what made them know whether they were in or out of alpha; they just "knew."

With the next experimental task, however, further enlightenment came. The subjects were now asked to try to produce the state called A on command—when a bell rang twice; when it rang once, they were to switch over to the state called B.

The amazing discovery was that the subjects had somehow learned by the preceding training how to put themselves onto either level.

This led to the next logical question: could people be taught to control their brain waves without this training, by themselves?

When Dr. Kamiya became associated with the Langley Porter Institute, he set up an electronic device that turned on a signal tone whenever alpha waves, or alpha, were present and turned off again the instant they weren't. Subjects were asked to try to maintain alpha as long as possible. They were also asked both to suppress alpha and to generate it, deliberately.

All the subjects were able to do so, and after a while, their descriptions of what the states felt like began to tally. A generation was achieved by a kind of passive blankness, a calming down of the mind, a release of judgments or questions, a mental letting-go. It was in some way very pleasant and preferable to the B state of suppression. Suppressing the A state, on the other hand, was easily achieved by visual imagery.

Some subjects showed EEG patterns similar to those found in twenty-year practitioners of Zazen (Zen meditation).

In the early 1970s, studies were undertaken by Drs. Robert Keith Wallace and Herbert Benson of the Harvard Medical School to further explore the physical correlates of Transcendental Meditation. These studies corroborated the presence of alpha brain waves and borderlines of theta brain waves during the extreme stillness of mind-body, and "restful alertness" of meditation, but this aspect will be gone into fully later in relation to training for higher states of consciousness.

This brings us now to the last biofeedback instrument in our list, and the most recent, the EEG machine, which we call the Mind Mirror because it does, in fact, *reflect* states of mind-body correlation.

The Mind Mirror is a form of electroencephalograph never produced before, and the story of its evolution in our research will be told later in more detail. Physically, the machine consists of twenty-four rows of light-emitting diodes (LEDs) arranged in two banks of twelve rows each. Each row comprises thirty-two LEDs, sixteen on the left bank, sixteen on the right, so that signals from both left and right hemispheres of the brain which are conducted via the electrodes and leads in the usual way can be shown up on the instrument at the same time and recorded and compared accordingly. For each hemisphere, there are twelve separate frequency channels.

With 16 LEDs in each of the 2 × 12 lines, there is a total of 384 subminiature lights, plus those in a thirteenth row (with lights of a different color which show up the presence of tension), making a total of 416 lights.

There is a separate amplifier for the signals in each frequency channel, which an integrated circuit converts to an illuminated display to make up the total pattern formation. In use, the Mind Mirror has a sufficiently rapid response

BRAINWAVE RHYTHMS

Despite all the differences of opinion which have been generated in the last ten years since the advent of relatively inexpensive biofeedback equipment, there has nevertheless been some measure of agreement about what the basic brain rhythms may mean:

Beta Rhythm:
13–30 Hz
(frequency measured in cycles per second)
The normal waking rhythm of the brain associated with active thinking or active attention, focusing on the outside world or solving concrete problems. The strength of the signal is increased by anxiety and reduced by muscular activity.

Alpha Rhythm:
8–13 Hz for adults,
4–7 Hz for children
Alpha is the most prominent rhythm in the whole realm of brain activity, but also the one with least apparent meaning unless the associated rhythms are also known. It denotes an empty mind rather than a relaxed one, a mindless state rather than a passive one. Most subjects produce some alpha with the eyes closed, and this is why it has been claimed that it is nothing but a kind of scanning or waiting pattern produced by the visual centers of the brain. It is usually reduced or eliminated by opening the eyes, hearing unfamiliar sounds, anxiety or mental concentration. Albert Einstein could solve complex mathematical problems while remaining in the alpha state, but our recent work suggests that this was not an alpha-alone state. One person in ten or twenty produces no alpha at all, while about one in ten produces alpha with the eyes open. Alpha per se is not associated with inwardly directed attention, relaxed awareness or feelings of well-being. These states seem to require the simultaneous presence of beta and theta for there to be any addition to the "no mind" state.

Theta Rhythm:

4–7 Hz

Alone, this frequency appears in dreaming or in the half-waking hypnagogic state with dreamlike imagery. Theta appears as consciousness slips toward drowsiness. Theta has been associated with access to unconscious material, creative inspiration and deep meditation, but these states will be found to be accompanied by other frequencies in the alpha and beta bands or with alpha alone in meditation.

Delta Rhythm:

½–4 Hz

Primarily associated with deep sleep. There have also been reports that delta waves appear at the onset of paranormal phenomena, and we find that they are also associated with the higher levels of consciousness.

time to enable the ephemeral brain-mind states to be seen, and patterns remain stable as long as the state is stable. They scatter the instant the state alters or breaks up. The subject can literally see not only the pattern of his state but how long he holds it and just what it becomes as it retreats.

The instrument uses electrodes attached to the head to pick up the voltages generated by the brain, and one of the advantages of the muscle-monitoring thirteenth row is that it eliminates the problem familiar to researchers of the intrusion of unwanted "parasitic" voltages such as those from facial, jaw or even scalp muscles.

The great sensitivity and ease of operation of the Mind Mirror, its wide frequency range (1.5 to 40 Hz) and above all its ability to show rhythms in both cerebral hemispheres at the same time, are already opening up the way to new discoveries and deeper understanding of the brain and its powerful and complex involvement with the body and health.

The latest addition to the Mind Mirror is the invaluable Data Recorder. For the remarkable visual patterns produced by the Mind Mirror to be acceptable to orthodox scientists and of practical use to clinicians, there needed to be some form of automatic, permanent record which could subsequently be examined and reexamined as necessary. This recording can now be made by means of a special cassette recorder.

Because data from conventional paper recorders are too bulky, and in the case of EEG recorders, might need computer facilities to convert them to a useful form, Geoffrey Blundell decided to use standard magnetic tape cassettes, recording the complex electrical signals in digital form (for full technical details see Appendix C).

Considerable other technical difficulties had to be overcome in connection with this choice, but the final result was that an hour or more of Mind Mirror patterns for two persons could be recorded together with ESR or myograph signals and elapsed time. It is a simple matter to correlate all this information with a recorded vocal commentary. The two persons whose parameters are recorded could, for example, be an experimenter and his subject or a healer and a patient.

Before coming to wider implications of all the foregoing, in the next chapter we will discuss the class and laboratory research leading up to the clear understanding of the need for such an instrument as the Mind Mirror, as well as some of the self-awareness training methods we employ to reach the higher states of consciousness.

Chapter 2

Recognizing
Internal States

The Research

The research with which this chapter is concerned may properly be considered to have begun in 1970, at which time, with Dr. Ann Woolley-Hart, we had for some two years been studying electrical skin resistance (ESR) as a possible clinical aid to diagnosis in preventive medicine for symptomless disease, that is, disease in its early stages before there are any overt symptoms.

We had experienced occasional difficulty due to the considerable variation which can occur when a subject is emotionally disturbed. From the viewpoint of the clinical project, this psychophysiological effect was merely a nuisance; but it then occurred to us that it might be exploited for the assessment of mental states, in lieu of the rather more usual method of the psychogalvanic reflex (PGR).

At the same time that we were involved in this work, we had been engaged in experimental hypnotic studies for which it was desirable to be able to monitor slow changes in the subject's state of mind and for which PGR measurements were unsuitable.

We knew that attempts to measure bodily correlates of mental states had been made for many years with varying degrees of success, and that electrical skin resistance had been among the methods used. For example, in 1930 M. Levine made an unsuccessful attempt to measure depth of hypnosis by ESR; in 1931 C. P. Richter carried out extensive experiments on change of ESR during sleep; and in 1960, Keith Wallace of Harvard Medical School used both ESR and electroencephalography (EEG) to study physiological effects of Transcendental Meditation, concluding that profound changes in bodily parameters do not occur in hypnosis; and many other workers had independently demonstrated that ESR is inversely related (meaning that as one factor becomes greater, another associated factor becomes smaller) to the level of neurological arousal.

Although there was an obvious inverse relationship between hypnosis and level of arousal (since a hypnotized subject, although he may be fully aware of his surroundings, is passive unless instructed otherwise), numerous recent studies had shown that hypnosis was accompanied by either an increase, a decrease or no change at all in ESR, heart rate, blood pressure or respiration. The conclusion reached by these workers that hypnosis had no reliable physiological correlate was disappointing, but Dr. Woolley-Hart had already established many causes of nonrepeatability in ESR measurements, several of which appeared to have been overlooked in some earlier work. It was decided, therefore, to make a pilot study of ESR in hypnotized subjects, applying all the precautions which had been found necessary in clinical work, to see whether any clear relationship could be found.

There was no difficulty in finding five experienced hypnotic subjects for the initial trials, and experiments were carried out on the relationship between ESR and level of arousal during trance. If subjects were unstressed, simply being given suggestions of relaxation and drowsiness and being permitted to stay in trance for a time and then awakened produced an ESR graph against time of a smooth curve. On the other hand, if subjects were stressed by being given tests of depth (e.g., asked to move a limb after being told that they were paralyzed, asked to solve problems in mental arithmetic or to recall events from childhood days), then the ESR varied widely. The greater the stress, the more nearly did the ESR approach its waking value.

These results strongly suggested that in hypnosis, as in sleep and in deep waking relaxation, the ESR *is* inversely proportional to the level of arousal. The problem then was how to explain the contradictory results obtained by other workers.

Despite our long experience of the complexities of making ESR measurements, we thought it improbable that other workers had neglected any simple physical factors. It seemed equally unlikely that the experimenters had been misled as to the depth of hypnosis of their subjects. The further possibility was that insufficient allowance had been made for personal psychophysiological factors such as the subject's temperament; any physical disease; whether he smoked, took drugs or alcohol; whether he had recently eaten or taken exercise; and so on. Emotional changes had been found to interfere with the measurement of bodily changes; it was quite clear that the reverse process must also occur.

A larger experimental series was planned with fourteen

subjects. To improve standardization and control, all the subjects were hypnotized by the same method, in the same room and as far as possible at the same time of day to reduce the effect of diurnal variations (variations that take place during the day, such as bodily temperature).

Before each session, notes were made for each subject as to whether he had recently taken exercise, eaten or smoked or taken any drugs. The value of this procedure was quickly proved: two of the new subjects started taking tranquilizers on medical advice, and they showed ESR values which were high both in absolute terms (i.e., as compared with the range of ESR values for people in general) and as compared with their readings before taking the drugs. During hypnosis, the ESR did increase above the waking value, but by a much smaller amount than usual; also, these subjects' response under stress was greatly reduced.

Before starting hypnosis, subjects were required to sit quietly with the electrodes in place for fifteen minutes. This also proved valuable: in cold weather, subjects who had just come in sometimes showed an initial *rise* of skin current. A similar effect sometimes occurred if the electrodes were very cold when first applied.

It is appropriate at this point to mention methods for distinguishing hypnosis from simulated hypnosis, and means for estimating trance depth. Simulation occasionally occurs, not because the subject wants to deceive the hypnotist, but because he is overanxious to cooperate and not let him down: this is an ever-present possibility which no experienced hypnotist neglects. Fortunately, there are several effective tests which can be applied. A hypnotized subject, told that he is being given eau de cologne to smell, for example, will sniff at ammonia appreciatively, whereas a simulator will be unable to hide his discomfort.

Since the earliest hypnotic experiments, psychologists have

tried to differentiate between the various depths of trance on the basis of the characteristic phenomena which could be elicited. In 1886 H. Bernheim described nine stages of hypnosis; A. A. Liebault in 1889, five; Auguste Forel in 1923 and others considered that three stages were enough for practical purposes. A very useful modern method is the LeCron-Bordeaux Scoring System, which takes into account fifty of the symptoms and sensations experienced by a hypnotized subject and scores two points for each symptom. Five stages are recognized: hypnoidal (just beginning to become suggestible), light trance, medium trance, deep trance and plenary (very deep) trance. Since subjects show great individual variation as to what symptoms they present (some deep trance symptoms may occasionally be manifested in light trance, and vice versa), no such scale is completely reliable. Nevertheless, the LeCron-Bordeaux System is a helpful guide, and we used it in our research for the main series of hypnotic experiments.

It was soon apparent that the person-to-person variation in average ESR and the session-to-session variation for each person made the measurement of absolute resistance values useless for the assessment of hypnotic depths. It was nevertheless quite clear that the ESR increased very rapidly as soon as the subject became hypnotized (especially in those subjects who had much experience of hypnosis and who had lost all nervousness).

In the pilot experiments, the measurements, which are made in microamperes (one-millionth of an ampere) of current through the body, were converted into electrical resistance (ohms) so as to obtain comparisons with the published results of other workers. In the main series, the work was simplified by recording and plotting current values. It was noticed that some subjects occasionally showed very low initial current values, usually when they were tired, and that in such instances, the total current fall during hypnosis might be only a few microamperes instead of the usual thirty or forty; and yet they were deeply hypnotized. The experimenters then realized that absolute values were no guide, but that what mattered was the *proportional* change that occurred on each occasion.

The result of plotting the greatest proportional current change in each of one hundred experimental trances against the maximum estimated depth of hypnosis, using the LeCron-Bordeaux Scoring System just described, reached in each trance session, showed there was considerable variation, and in view of the difficulty of assessing depth of hypnosis from bodily symptoms, as well as the difficulty of obtaining an ESR reading uninfluenced by extraneous factors, was only to be expected. The agreement, however, was good enough to show that measurement of ESR could be a most valuable tool for monitoring hypnotic trance depth.

The most striking feature was something which could not be shown in tabular form and had to be experienced to be appreciated: it was the extent to which the use of an ESR meter improved hypnotic rapport. Every smallest change in the subject's state is immediately indicated, and the hypnotist has a clear guide to his progress—and his mistakes. For instance, we were hypnotizing a patient for the first time, and after a good start, suggested, "As I count slowly from one to ten, your sleep will become progressively deeper, much deeper." As soon as counting began, the meter showed great agitation (a rapid oscillation), followed by the patient beginning to wake up (a rapid fall in the ESR). The patient was awakened and questioned. It transpired that he had been a parachutist, and counting slowly was, to him, a very exciting procedure!

Induction was repeated, using the letters of the alphabet in place of counting, and deep trance was reached in ten minutes. Apart from the help with induction, therefore, we saw that rapport is improved because the subject is impressed by the hypnotist's ability to say, "No, drop that thought, it is disturbing to you. Just relax, and let it go."

For many years, we had been of the opinion that a large part of the beneficial effects of hypnotherapy, and even of psychoanalysis, was due to the long periods of deep relaxation on the therapist's couch, a view which was strengthened by what we learned about sensory deprivation (described in more detail later) during visits in 1963 and 1964 to McGill and Princeton universities. When Dr. Woolley-Hart, in the spring of 1972, seriously questioned the relative effectiveness of suggestion and of deep relaxation in hypnotherapy, we immediately began to design an experiment.

In the autumn of 1972, with two groups of volunteers (usually twenty in each group), we tried the effect on group A of ten weekly sessions of two hours each in which, after a short paper had been read on some aspect of psychosomatic health, the class received group hypnotherapy in the form of simple suggestions for health and confidence. The B group also heard the same paper on psychosomatic health, followed by an hour or more of autogenic exercises and deep psycho-physiological relaxation, that is, relaxation deep enough to produce a 250 percent or greater increase in ESR. No suggestions of health were given (other than that implicit in the situation), but this group showed great benefits compared with the others.

This therapeutic effect, we agreed, was due to the shift from sympathetic nervous system activity to parasympathetic activity, from the fight-or-flight response to the relaxation response, which resulted from the technique used. (Yogis have known for thousands of years that very deep relaxation can be produced by concentrating upon particular images.) We then studied both hypnotized subjects and subjects experiencing "led" meditation and found that the depth of the relaxation response was related to the characteristics of the suggested imagery. After extensive studies of both ESR changes and bilateral EEG patterns on more than one hundred subjects, we found that a succession of brief word pictures, each of about 150 to 200 words and of varied content, would reliably produce in the majority of subjects a faster and deeper relaxation response than traditional induction methods.

In order to confirm the validity of these initial results in a convincing manner, it was necessary to experiment with much larger numbers of subjects—several hundred at least—and the first task was to set up courses in self-control of internal states. The methods used would include biofeedback training, autogenic exercises, meditation, creative reverie and hypnagogic imagery—all well-established arts. Variations on the theme of deep psychophysiological relaxation could then be tested on classes of fifteen to twenty subjects at a time, who would learn to relax properly and, hopefully, would gain much else besides.

Our main concern at that time was the development of a background physiological plan. Interest in and experience with meditation and other Oriental arts had convinced us both of their efficacy and of the strength of Western opposition to such ideas. From the outset, we decided that a good deal of effort must go into the verification of the health benefits on strictly scientific lines, but of equal importance was the development of an acceptable theory of mind-body interaction.

Almost nine months of preliminary studies and experiments with volunteers went into the design of Maxwell Cade's Basic Course, the premise of which was that a fundamental distinction existed and must be clearly maintained between training in self-control of autonomic nervous system responses (the fight-or-flight response and the relaxation response) and training in self-awareness and self-control of the differential functions of the two hemispheres of the brain.

Two courses were therefore designed. Part 1, Psychocybernetics, or mind control, which concentrated on self-awareness of levels of arousal and the development of control over the fight-or-flight response and the relaxation response (explained more fully in the next chapter), and Part 2, Psychotechnics, a term used in humanistic psychology to mean "teaching people to develop their full potential," which concentrated upon mental imagery and development of full awareness of the differential functions of the two cerebral hemispheres.

For the courses to succeed in their intended purpose of teaching people self-control through self-awareness, biofeedback equipment of various kinds would be needed, but—and this was a serious difficulty—there appeared to be no equipment on the market at that time (the winter of 1972) that would meet the requirements. Most ESR meters gave an audible tone as their output and therefore were incapable of absolute measurements, while electroencephalographs were little more than alpha-theta indicators, giving no measurement of either signal strength or frequency.

We therefore designed and made our own ESR equipment, but the special EEG was a far more complex requirement. A design for an EEG which would measure the amplitude and frequency of the alpha, beta, theta and delta rhythms from both hemispheres of the brain was roughed out and then more fully developed with the help of the late Dr. W. Grey Walter of the Burden Neurological Institute, but no one could be found to undertake the actual construction. Consequently, when the classes began in London in June,

1973, the only EEG available was a commercial instrument of very limited performance. (All this was to change when, six months later, Geoffrey Blundell, the proprietor of Audio Limited, joined one of the classes and expressed interest in manufacturing biofeedback apparatus.)

The absence of suitable EEGs meant that the first five or six ten-week courses yielded little information on the two hemispheres of the brain, but a great deal of valuable information was obtained from the ESR instruments. It was this information on which the Self-Measurement of Neurophysical Type was eventually based.

The use of the ESR meters, which were read at frequent intervals during each trance session, also made possible the compilation of the table of Subjective and Objective Correlates of Stages of Relaxation and the Lesh numbers, based upon the Response Patterns to Meditation reported by Terry V. Lesh in 1970. The responses of our students and subjects were not quite the same as those of Terry V. Lesh's students at the University of Oregon, of course, and our idea of adding objective correlates to the subjective feelings of the mediators was therefore evolved.

In June, 1974, we drew up the first table of subjective meditative states based upon ESR measurements on 120 pupils and EEG observations on 70 pupils. The values given on pp. 40–41, which was drawn up in October, 1976, are based upon subsequent ESR and EEG observations of more than one thousand subjects.

By far the most important concept derived from the early (1972–1974) observations was that of the Two-Correlate Graph of Altered States of Consciousness (p. 42), which we first described in November, 1974, to the Society for Psychosomatic Research at the Royal College of Physicians in London. We had long believed that no single physiological correlate could adequately represent an altered state of con-

Parameter	Self-Measurement of Neurophysical Type				
	Very tense	Mildly overaroused	Normal range	Very relaxed	Under- aroused
1. **Absolute resistance**	20K or below	40K to 80K	100K to 200K	220K to 280K	300K or above
2. **Response to challenge in %**	200% or more	140% to 160%	about 100%	40% to 60%	below 25%
3. **Time for return after challenge in seconds**	more than 150	100 to 120	about 90	50 to 60	about 20
4. **Spontaneous fluctuations in reading**	many violent	a few strong ones	a few weak ones	none	none

sciousness but were pleasantly surprised at the information which the two-correlate graph gave.

Referring to the chart on page 117, one sees that the frequency of the dominant brain rhythm is displayed along the horizontal axis and change in ESR along the vertical axis. The first information the graph provides is a grouping of all states of consciousness into four categories:

1. Aroused body–aroused mind. Low ESR–beta EEG. Ordinary waking states, extending in the extreme upper right corner to panic states.

2. Relaxed body–relaxed mind. High ESR–alpha or alpha-theta EEG. States of sleep, reverie and meditation.

3. Aroused body–relaxed mind. Low ESR–alpha or alpha-theta EEG. Ecstatic states, mediumistic trance, somnambulism.

4. Relaxed body–alert mind. High ESR–alpha, beta and theta EEG. Zen meditation.

A typical waking movement is represented by a diagonal movement on the graph from corner 2 to corner 1. When mind and body arousals are displaced relative to each other, we have states of disassociation in which there often seem to be a splitting of consciousness. Lines of constant dissociation are lines drawn parallel to the main diagonal on the graph.

Although we were not able to develop fully our scheme of EEG correlates of different levels of consciousness until the first Mind Mirror became available in June, 1976, the idea of a hierarchy of levels of consciousness based upon purely biological evidence occurred to us in the summer of 1974, when the first of the improved EEG Monitor equipment became available.

While these machines did not have a visual display like the subsequent Mind Mirror, they did provide channels for left and right brain hemispheres, gave an indication of the signal strength and provided a frequency meter which made it possible to read the alpha, theta or beta frequency to an accuracy of 5 percent.

It was the EEG Monitor which made it possible to observe

changes in a subject's bilateral EEG pattern throughout a series of altered states of consciousness. And it was in the very first term, using these instruments, that we made our most important observation: that whenever a subject or student showed remarkable mind-body control, he always showed the peculiar bilaterally symmetrical EEG pattern which later we came to regard as characteristic of a level of consciousness beyond the "fourth state" of meditation.

At the same time (June–August, 1974), there were among our two hundred pupils at the Franklin School in London a number of experienced meditators. There were two practitioners of Zazen with several years' experience and ten practitioners of Transcendental Meditation (TM) with experience ranging from one to nine years, as well as some American students with experience of various different schools. All the experienced meditators, no matter what their background training, showed the same general pattern of brain waves during meditation: bilaterally symmetrical alpha, the frequency of which steadily decreased as meditation deepened, then a steadily strengthening bilateral theta accompaniment.

Some private patients, practicing deep reverie under supervision, also showed very symmetrical EEG patterns although according to their ESRs, they were not very deep. It began to look as if asymmetry of the EEG pattern in normal people was largely a characteristic of the waking state. This was not surprising if, as current theory proposes, the specialization of the two brain hemispheres has been developed to facilitate response to the environment. One would expect that in the active waking state, with attention focused on the external world, the activities of the two hemispheres would differ, whereas in more internally focused states, there might be more integration.

It seems to have been thought from the earliest times that

SUBJECTIVE AND OBJECTIVE CORRELATES OF STAGES OF RELAXATION

Lesh number	Subjective Correlates of State	Relaxation microamps	Response % change	EEG Rhythms as seen on the Mind Mirror
0	Just beginning to relax. Subject may report difficulty in stilling the mind: the itchy state. Why am I doing this?	25 to 20	below 25%	intermittent alpha and beta
1	Subjects have reported feeling dizzy or having befogged consciousness or sensation like going under an anesthetic. You may find yourself filling your mind with everyday affairs, almost as an avoidance of meditation. Don't focus on the feelings, just let go. Imagine this stage of the meditation as an inverted pyramid with the flat top representing the scattered energies of the self and the tip of this inverted pyramid as the one pointed focus toward which the meditation flows.	20 to 16	25% to 35% approx.	reduced beta continuous alpha

2	Calmness and relaxation. Childhood or other scenes from the past recalled as "flashbacks." Attention need not be very sustained.	16 to 13	35% to 45%	continuous alpha no beta intermittent theta
3	Well defined state. Pleasant bodily sensations of floating, lightness, rocking, swaying (subjects may actually move rhythmically). More sustained concentration. Increased and clearer imagery.	13 to 10	45% to 55%	continuous alpha with falling frequency almost continuous theta
4	Extremely vivid awareness of breathing, heartbeat, or other bodily sensations. Effortless concentration. Sometimes a sensation of "being full of air" or of "growing to great size." Sometimes an alternation between internal and external awareness.	10 to 8	60% to 70%	continuous alpha theta falling in frequency
5	Very lucid state of consciousness. Deeply satisfying. Intense alertness, calmness and detachment. Feeling of altered state lacking in previous levels 0 to 4.	8 to 5	70% to 80%	continuous theta alpha frequency near the theta border
6	New way of feeling, one has intuitive insight perhaps into old problems, as though seen from a more aware level. Synthesis of opposites into a higher unity.	below 4	over 80%	very little electrical brain activity except occasional delta

TWO-CORRELATE GRAPH OF
ALTERED STATES OF CONSCIOUSNESS

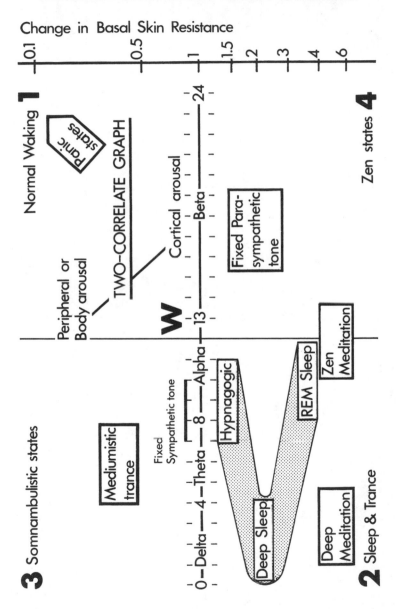

Change in Basal Skin Resistance

Normal Waking **1**

Zen states **4**

Panic states

TWO-CORRELATE GRAPH

Peripheral or Body arousal

Cortical arousal

Beta

Fixed Para-sympathetic tone

W

Mediumistic trance

Fixed Sympathetic tone

Alpha

Hypnagogic

Theta

Delta

Deep Sleep

REM Sleep

Zen Meditation

Deep Meditation

3 Somnambulistic states

2 Sleep & Trance

man has within him some dormant, unmanifest, divine power which, once awakened, could transform him from common clay to an intellectual giant, a compassionate saint and a master of wisdom. Usually this transformation has been seen as so vast as to require a number of intermediate stages. Ideas as to the possible number of levels of consciousness have varied very widely, and the following are only given as examples:

Dr. Richard Bucke	3
P. D. Ouspensky	4
R. S. De Ropp	5
Dr. Anthony Campbell (based on the Maharishi Mahesh Yogi)	7
John C. Lilly	9
Durand Kiefer	15

Durand Kiefer's list includes various states such as pain, neurosis, headache and blank, which, while they are arguably distinct states of mind, clearly do not constitute a hierarchy. Dr. Lilly's list comprises one neutral state and three positive and three negative states. All these lists (and the innumerable others to be found in the literature) are what one might term subjective lists, being based upon various persons' different subjective experiences. We realized early in this work that what was required was some kind of objective hierarchy, one in which the various levels could be identified by some unique physiological pattern.

By the summer of 1974, with the use of several of the new Audio EEG Monitors, we were able to verify the patterns of sleep, reverie and meditation established by other workers, and to begin a study of the different forms of waking consciousness and had made our first observations of what we then termed Lucid Awareness and later called the Awakened Mind.

None of these patterns could be claimed to be more than indications, because reading the frequency scale of the EEG Monitors, switching from beta to alpha and theta, then repeating the whole procedure for the opposite hemisphere was a time-consuming operation taking from one to one and a half minutes, during which the pattern might have altered. This was the point where we began pressing Geoffrey Blundell to produce a prototype, no matter how crude, of a visual-display EEG which would show patterns of the electrical activity of both brain hemispheres over a wide frequency spectrum and in real time.

While Geoffrey Blundell began the complex, technically challenging design work, we continued studies of the bilateral rhythms of students in our classes, of private patients and of healers and their patients. Without a real-time display, which would show transient patterns as well as more stable states of brain activity, we could not ascertain whether or not brain rhythms would prove to be our long-sought physiological correlate of hierarchical states of consciousness. We did, however, make one promising observation: whereas deep sleep, dreaming sleep, the hypnagogic state and the waking state (see chart) all seemed to be accompanied by a single band of EEG frequencies (respectively delta, theta, alpha and beta), the meditative states appeared to be accompanied by two or more frequency bands.

It was of course known that the EEG rhythm could be analyzed and the result expressed as a complex spectral diagram; A. R. Luria, in *The Walking Brain*, shows such diagrams in response to stimuli. These diagrams look like half of the Mind Mirror display, but they were not produced as they were happening—in real time—and therefore the subjective correlation was not easy to verify.

OBJECTIVELY CORRELATED LEVELS OF CONSCIOUSNESS PRIOR TO MIND MIRROR

5	Fifth State—Goleman Afterglow—Maharishi Illumination—Fromm Lucid Awareness—Cade	suggested —still subjective	
4	Fourth State—Wallace Meditation—traditional Relaxation Response		
3	Waking Waking Sleep—Gurdjieff		
2	Hypnagogic State	(between waking and sleeping)	
	Hypnopompic State	(between sleeping and waking)	
1	Dreaming Sleep	(aware of dream content) also lucid dreaming—aware	
	Deep Sleep	aware of nothing	

We will return to the work on levels of consciousness later, but at this point, it should be noted that the work on brain rhythms had an essentially orthodox approach. It is a widespread scientific assumption that consciousness is produced by the activity of the brain, and therefore the activity of consciousness is identical with brain activity. This assumption is known as the psychoneural identity thesis. Because the whole universe is compounded of matter and energy of a purely physical nature, say the materialists, consciousness itself must be a result of physical activity of some kind. All the beauty and mystery of poetical and religious thought simply represent complex patterns of the firing of neurons in the brain and nervous system.

As long as the hierarchy of states is based on each person's necessarily limited experience, then it is vulnerable to attack from the psycho-neural identity thesis. But as soon as one can discern an order in the states of consciousness governed by a single principle such as increasing integration, then one is entitled to see this as a study not of matter but of mind.

The Classes

Our background plan for psychophysiological training in Self-Control Through Self-Awareness was first to teach self-awareness of autonomic nervous system responses and then to give training in self-awareness of the differential functions of the two hemispheres of the brain. The scheme was based in part upon theoretical considerations of the neurophysiological relation between the nervous system and bodily functioning and the neuropsychological relation between the nervous system and mental functioning processes which it seemed desirable to be able to control, and in part upon what seemed to be the aim of much of the training of various schools of martial arts.

Awareness of Arousal

In the very first session of the Basic Course, the participants were given a guided meditation or, more accurately, a guided exercise in imagery in which they were asked, for instance, to accompany the leader on an imaginary country walk (see Some Examples of Guided Imagery Exercises and Other Self-Biofeedback Aids at end of chapter). This served two purposes: (a) to develop an awareness of imaging ability; and (b) to develop awareness of arousal level. The subjects' imagery was (and continues to be) evaluated on the Sheehan Scale (p. 48), and it was made very clear that they were to rate the most vivid images they had, *without regard for whether or not they were relevant to the theme given by the leader.*

True hypnagogic imagery tends to be vivid, changeable, unpredictable and transient. As far as imagery is concerned, guided imagery is merely an occasion for the student to experience his own capacity for spontaneous images. Training in control of images comes much later. At the end of the exercise, the students were asked to slowly open their eyes and look at their meters. "Don't try to read it accurately," they were instructed, "but notice how the needle moves to the right when you start to take big, deep breaths. . . . Start your big breaths now."

Later they were asked to compare their subjective feelings during the exercise with the Table of Subjective Meditative States.

During the eighth seminar, the students were suddenly instructed to "think about your level of arousal. . . . Don't look at your meters, but estimate what they *should* be reading. . . . Imagine what it would feel like to be just twice as relaxed as you now are. . . . What would your meter then be reading? Now you don't have to *do* anything . . . just let it happen."

A five-minute guided adventure is then given (see section on guided imagery and other aids to self-biofeedback at end of chapter) while the students gradually become twice as relaxed. Usually, three-quarters of the class double their depth of relaxation within 15 to 20 percent and can be consid-

SHEEHAN'S MENTAL IMAGERY SCALE (1967)

	Rating
Perfectly clear and as vivid as the actual experience	1
Very clear and comparable in vividness to the actual experience	2
Moderately clear and vivid	3
Not clear or vivid but recognizable	4
Vague and dim	5
So vague and dim as to be hardly recognizable	6
No image present at all, only knowing that you're thinking of the object	7

NOTE: As applied to the Visualization Sequences, this scale has to be matched to (1) visual imagery, (2) touch, pain, heat and cold (skin senses), (3) taste and smell, (4) sound, and (5) kinesthesia (sensation of bodily movement). The score can vary, therefore, from $5 \times 1 = 5$ to $5 \times 7 = 35$, where the higher the score, the poorer the mental imagery. *The ability to think in sensory images instead of in words is an absolutely essential first step toward the mastery of higher states of consciousness, self-control of pain, etc.*

ered to have completed this first part of their training to that stage. The other quarter will need some additional help to increase their self-awareness.

We now come to another biofeedback device: strobe lighting. Before the classes began, we were looking for a suitable lamp to emit flashes of red light over a range of frequencies corresponding to the theta and alpha brain rhythms (i.e., four to twelve flashes per second). Dr. W. Grey Walter, in a private communication, had advised us of the usefulness of such photic stimulation for the development of imagery, and Professor John Wallace, during one of our visits to Jefferson University in Philadelphia, had mentioned the American work on strobe lighting as a powerful way to enhance memory.

There were known risks with the use of such flickering lights with persons who might be susceptible to epileptic fits, but we reasoned that such risks could be reduced to a very low level if subjects were only exposed to the lights after they had become very relaxed, and during the first few exposures a close watch was kept on their ESR meters for signs of abnormal arousal. After four years' use of the lights, with more than four thousand pupils including twenty-five known epileptics, there have been no mishaps, and most of the epileptics have reported a marked improvement in their condition.

The effects of the strobe lighting on pupils' memory and creativity have been remarkable (and since the Mind Mirrors became available it has been possible to study the exact effect strobe lighting has upon the subjects' brain waves). Primarily, the effect seemed to be a stabilization and synchronization of both hemispheres, and this effect, when once produced, seemed to be of long duration. Despite the evidently beneficial effects, we warn that strobe lighting is not a method to be employed without all necessary precautions.

By this time, we had begun to suspect that the "higher mind," on the neuropsychological level, was what Carl Jung called transcendent function, and that it was manifested by the integration of left- and right-hemisphere functions in an uninhibited, reciprocal transmission of nervous impulses across the corpus callosum, the great bridge of nervous tissue which unites the two halves of the brain. This, we reasoned further, would to a great extent provide the union of conscious with unconscious mental contents; the integration of the left hemisphere's extroverted, verbal, rational and abstract processes with the right hemisphere's introverted, visual-spatial, synthetic and holistic (wholes that are more than the sum of their constituent parts) patterns.

First it was necessary to devise some exercises by which the student could become aware of the feeling of left-brain and right-brain types of activity, or, to be more accurate, types of mental activity in which either left-hemisphere or right-hemisphere functions predominated.

Bearing in mind the limitations of the classroom situation, we designed word pictures that could be used for right-hemisphere activity and word games for left-hemisphere activity. To increase the contrast, they were alternated, as the following example shows:

1. (RH) I want you to see yourself as a flower. What kind of flower are you? Can you clearly see your stem, leaves, petals, roots? Where do you grow? Are you growing wild or in a well-kept garden? What other flowers, shrubs or trees grow near you? Is the weather good or bad? Do you experience any trouble from worms, insects, animals or birds? Do not rationalize; just feel all these things by trying your best to *be* a flower for the next few minutes . . .

2. (LH) Now, change *bull* into *gate*. Write down the word *bull,* then, changing one letter at a time, change *bull* into *gate* (bull-gull-gall-gale-gate). Now, in the same way, turn *rich* into *poor,* each step being a word.

These simple exercises seemed to be very effective in giving pupils the feeling of the two modes of mental activity, but it was not until the Mind Mirror was available that the difference in bilateral power spectrum (that is, the relative levels of energy in the theta, alpha and beta wave bands on the two sides of the head) could be clearly demonstrated.

Another example of the contrast between right- and left-hemisphere activities is given by the following exercise, but it must be remembered that it is not how well one does in the exercise itself that matters but how well one can assess one's own subjective feelings while trying to do the exercise:

1. (RH) Imagine vividly the color red . . . orange . . . yellow . . . green . . . blue . . . indigo . . . violet. . . . Now, the *feel* of stroking a soft, furry kitten . . . a handful of wet sand . . . an ice cube. . . . The *smell* or *taste* of an autumn bonfire . . . roasting coffee beans . . . fresh lemon juice . . . hot tar. . . . The *sound* of surf on a shingle beach . . . a cock crowing at dawn . . . thunder . . . hail on the windowpanes. . . . The *bodily sensations* of being in a fast elevator which stops suddenly . . . being on a swing . . . climbing a steep flight of stairs. . . .

2. (LH) Mentally add one plus two minus three plus four minus five plus six minus seven plus eight. . . . Now mentally solve this problem: what is three-quarters of seven sevens less five fives?

Our next step was to try and learn more of the hypnagogic state. A great deal has been written about its importance. Elmer and Alyce Green, at the Menninger Institute, have particularly contributed to our knowledge of how alpha-theta EEG biofeedback can be used to develop people's awareness of the feeling of this state so that it may be turned on at will. We felt that it was important to start work on this state as early in the course as possible and without the time-consuming process of EEG training.

As a means suitable for classroom use, we put a buzzer and a small battery in a plastic box which could be held comfortably in one hand. There was an on-off switch and a push button. When the device was switched on, the buzzer

sounded unless the button was depressed. These "hypnagogostats" (our term for them) proved very effective.

A classroom of beginners sat with these instruments in
their laps and tried to relax while it was explained to them
that, at a critical state of relaxation, images begin to arise in
the mind, and that at that time, it would become very difficult to maintain pressure on the button.

Usually there was some difficulty in getting a class to relax
sufficiently without assistance, and for this we used two
methods: (a) a cassette player softly playing familiar music
(Rimski-Korsakov's *Scheherazade*, for example), which
usually caused an increasing number of buzzers to sound
within a few minutes, and (b) the class leader intoning the
"sensory sequences" (see section at end of chapter), which
produces rather different results. There were some key sensations, for instance, which usually resulted in almost every
buzzer coming on at once.

Many students speak of vivid pictures appearing suddenly
into their minds. "I was still aware of the room around me,"
said one. "The buzzer seemed to jerk me into awareness of
pictures which I didn't know were there, as if one part of
my mind had the pictures, and another part—more like
me—became consciously aware of them." Many students became so pleased with their experiences that they bought or
made hypnagogostats for themselves and subsequently reported continued good results.

Mental fluency was another element of our self-awareness
classes. It may be defined as the ability to readily manipulate
one's mental contents, both as to quality (words, images,
feelings, music) and quantity (the sorting of facts and figures
against an imminent deadline, or the almost mindlessness of
an alpha state). It is obvious that mental fluency is a skill and
that not all people possess it in the same degree, but it was
not until we had been running our classes for almost a year

that we realized how widely people differed. One couple, married for more than ten years, suddenly realized that the woman thought in vivid spatial images and the man thought only in complex verbal constructs; it explained much about their unresolved differences.

A surprising number of students had virtually no visual imagery, but even more surprising was the number who had great difficulty manipulating images and more or less had to make do with whatever popped into their minds. A considerable number—and not specifically old or young, male or female—found certain kinds of imagery not just unattractive but almost unbearable. It became clear that, for these people, some training in imagery manipulation was essential.

Imagery manipulation is primarily a function of the right hemisphere; it is also more effective at low levels of arousal. This aspect of training was therefore deferred until the second half of the basic course ("psychotechnics"). In each of the ten seminars comprising the course, a twenty-minute period was devoted to a guided meditation specifically designed to strengthen the pupils' ability to handle complex, stressful and even frightening images. Some examples are as follows:

1. Manipulation of Body Image. Seeing one's self as very large and very small; very heavy (made of lead) and very light (made of vapor).

2. Shamanistic Experiences. Seeing one's real self leave the body and inhabit the body of an animal or bird, perhaps in some far-distant land.

3. Controlling Nightmares. In a nightmare situation, overcoming monsters and dangerous physical situations by manipulating the environment. It is stressed that the use of the creative imagination is to be developed for application to real-life problems.

4. Development and Perfection of Body Image. Seeing the body as something separate from you. Examining its defects dispassionately. Seeing a new body image, particularly as being vigorously healthy and free from defects. Seeing one's self occupying the new body.

5. Preparation for Mystical Experience. On a country walk, in woodlands, or on a mountainside. Gradually melting into the environment, losing all feeling of separateness or difference, becoming one with the universe.

6. Development of Empathy. Each subject has to imagine a bubble which just encloses him or her at head and heel and which represents both the consciousness and the "personal space." These bubbles then have to be expanded slowly so as to include the consciousness of more and more of the group, until eventually there is only one bubble of group consciousness. Subjects then withdraw the consciousness slowly to themselves, and note whether there is a sense of relief at the return to privacy or a sense of loss at the breakup of group empathy. They are not required to reveal their feelings to the group.

The whole group then undergoes an imaginary adventure together (climbing a mountain, exploring a tropical forest, crossing a polar ice cap, journeying into outer space).

Inevitably, some students had better results than others, and there were individual reactions to consider. A policy was adopted of finding for the more successful performers those consciousness-altering exercises that most facilitated their entry into higher states. This proved difficult to do with the present equipment, and it was not until we had the Mind Mirror to open up our research that we were able to pin down some very elusive factors.

Once our students were connected to the Mind Mirrors, we quickly found that before any pupil entered a very deep meditative state, and remained in that state for any length of time at all, this transformation was almost invariably preceded by a number of very transient appearances of the pattern of some higher state.

These brief "awakenings," so to speak, lasted for five seconds or less, and therefore were impossible to observe with the ordinary EEG monitors. Sometimes a few transient patterns in each of the three or four seminars preceded the appearance of a full-blown State Five, or Lucid Awareness, as we called it, lasting half an hour or more. More usually, the transient patterns would slowly increase in duration (up to fifteen or twenty seconds) over several terms (four or five months) before going suddenly into the prolonged higher state. The training for this state was repeated as necessary.

The poorer performers were encouraged to spend more time in simple alpha/theta training, relying on the well-established principle that the more these states are experienced, the easier they are to produce at will. Subjects were asked to use the EEG training equipment to the full, switching themselves from alpha training to theta training and from left hemisphere to right hemisphere until they could produce a high level of sustained alpha or theta activity in both hemispheres. From time to time, a trained operator would check progress and also monitor beta- and delta-wave activity, entering all the findings in the class book for the sake of completeness of records.

Great care was taken to avoid developmental "forcing," that is, attempting to push students or subjects beyond their stage of progress. They were not given training for Fifth State consciousness until they had shown their ability to attain it spontaneously during or after meditation sessions. It was quickly apparent that there is a difference between the first appearances of the alpha-beta-theta triad in the meditative, quietly seated condition and the ability to hold the same pattern of brain activity while fully active.

But before going on to consider this and other elements that have emerged from Fifth State or Lucid Awareness training, we would first like to elaborate on aspects fundamental to its very existence.

Some Examples of Guided Imagery Exercises and Other Self-Biofeedback Aids

The purpose of this section is to provide a few of the guided-imagery exercises we use in class and to suggest ways in which self-awareness and self-control, even the higher states of awareness, can be developed by those who do not have the machines.

Along with the guided adventures and the sensory exercises here, we draw your attention to the fact that there are several other forms of exercises (e.g., Ouspensky's exercises in self-awareness on pp. 109–110, together with the meditation-breathing exercises that follow on pp. 111–112) that can be done without the machines. And even though the majority of exercises given throughout the book are in conjunction with the biofeedback instruments, this does not necessarily mean they cannot be done without them.

The prime difference between self-awareness training with or without machines is that the former greatly reduces the time required to gain the deep state of relaxation that leads on to good meditation, often provides more precise motivation due to the immediate confirmation ("Oh, look, I am actually doing it, controlling my brain wave rhythm, affecting the needle!") and aids that vital suspension of disbelief that opens the way to firsthand experience and self-evidence of results.

On the other hand, it must never be overlooked that the latter method, without machines, has been carried out for countless centuries without technological assistance. Mainly, you use a machine in order to learn the subjective feeling of carrying out a certain operation, and later on, when you want to carry out that operation, you remember the subjective feeling and reconstruct it. There's no real difference between how we do it, using biofeedback instruments, and how a yogi does it, carrying out unquestioningly the instructions of his guru. Equally, there must be a suspension of disbelief until experience, or enlightenment, is self-known, beyond doubt, beyond precise explanation in words.

In doing these exercises, there can be no step-by-step technique. To tell you how you should or should not feel would be to negate the principle of self-experience. Each guided imagery, for instance, is for each individual a quite separate and incomparable experience. Here is where individuality most shows itself, for it is how *you* feel, how *you* react, what *you* sense and see, what *you* experience that unfolds your self-awareness to you, to the only one that matters.

The main object is to remember, later to recognize, and gradually to realize and expand your self-awareness into self-control and eventually the development of the higher states described later in this book. And the only way you will be able to judge your achievement is by the ways in which the states and feelings affect you, by the subsequent changes in your personality and in your attitudes to life (aspects which are gone into fully later). If you feel more alive, more creative, more at peace, steadier and calmer, more understanding of others and yourself, less likely to be rattled, kinder, more open and at ease, then you can be sure you're making progress. Above all, if you feel *compelled*, when you are at time thrown off course, to go and sit quietly and do your relaxation work, you will continue to progress.

While the guided adventures given here are available on tape (see Appendix), you may also read them off onto tape yourself, then play them back. They are most effective when read slowly in a soft, distinct tone without too much variation. It may be best to make a preliminary recording and then sit quietly and listen to it to decide whether it was too slow or too fast for you. As a general rule, somewhere between 100 and 115 words per minute is about the right speed, but some like it a little faster, some considerably slower. If the last is so, the words should not be spread out, but more intervals allowed between sentences.

Basically, guided imagery is most helpful in developing mental fluency (that is, flexibility of imagination for stimulating creativity, for loosening one from the tight grip of the so-called normal state which we are conditioned to believe is the most desirable, imposing its rigid limits on our self-development.

In order to gain the most from these adventures (and always, of course, from meditation), it is essential that you be as relaxed as possible. Without the machines as guide, it would be useful to use either Ainslie Meare's relaxation sequence given on page 87 or the Schultz Autogenic sequence on page 76.

Beginners in our classes who haven't got instruments at home are always told they will have some homework to do: to become distinctly aware of the difference between a tense and a relaxed body. It is just as important to recognize the relaxed state of well-being as it is the points of tension that may have worked up in your muscles, responding to tension in your thoughts and emotions. In this regard, there is nothing simpler than Edmund Jacobson's "progressive relaxation."

This amounts to spending ten minutes a day just lying on

the floor or on a firm couch, tensing up the muscles of one arm, letting it go completely, comparing it with the other, thinking about the difference for five or ten minutes. That's all. Next day, do it with the other arm, the next with one leg raised well up in the air, toes pointed down hard, thighs tightening, then shaking the whole leg out. And then do it with the stomach muscles, and the chest muscles, and the shoulder muscles, finally ending up with perhaps just one of the fingers on a hand.

When you have the feeling that you are sufficiently relaxed, by whatever means you have adopted, then sit down comfortably, remembering that it is important to keep your back straight; it must never be rigid or tense, just straight, and it's preferable not to lean against anything. Now, letting go of your thinking, feeling tranquil and deeply quiet, you are ready to begin your guided-imagery adventures.

Although all forms of meditation (and this is only one of them) are beneficial, we suggest that they are even more so done in a group. If you can find some like-minded people to share the experience, it will have the effect of deepening the mood and atmosphere for all.

Ultimately, the aim is to become as self-aware as possible, to remember what you have experienced and felt, and to carry over the relaxed, meditative state into your daily life.

Some of the guided-imagery exercises given here are for one person, some for groups. They are not graded for difficulty, nor are they progressive. Each is a separate experience.

THE GREEN DOOR FANTASY

I want you to come with me now upon a journey. I don't know quite where it will take us, but we will start off from the Round Pond in Kensington Gardens and make our way toward the Serpentine, down a long grassy avenue, tall trees on either side, quite a few birds about, a lot of gray squirrels, hardly any people. . . .

We keep count of the trees as we pass, one, two, three, four, five, six, seven, eight, nine, ten, eleven, twelve, thirteen, fourteen, fifteen, sixteen, seventeen, eighteen, nineteen, twenty, somewhere along here is what we're looking for—a bit further on, possibly—twenty-nine, thirty, thirty-one. . . .

Ah, here we are, this tree, the big broad one, has a little green doorway in its trunk. We go inside quickly before anyone can see us, and we find ourselves on a brightly lit spiral stairway that leads straight down into the ground. . . .

We start off on a little wrought-iron platform, and after every fifteen steps, we come to another little platform. We'll count the platforms, because it's somewhere around the tenth or twelfth that we want; but the platforms themselves are interesting. On each one, there's a shop. The shop must somehow be accommodated within the thick bark of the tree. . . .

I don't know how that can happen, but they're fascinating shops. This one is an old-fashioned sweet shop, with a window full of homemade candy, humbugs, sticks of rock with bright spiral colors on them, all sorts of lovely old-fashioned sweets. And then on the second platform, we come to a gunsmith, and there are old dueling pistols in the window, and also swords and suits of armor, but mainly dueling pistols, fowling pieces, weapons of that sort. . . .

The next one is a drugstore, a real old-fashioned apothecary, with great bottles of colored fluid in the windows—blue, amethyst, gold, bright red. . . .

And now there's an old curiosity shop full of the most extraordinary variety of items from bygone days—mugs and patchwork quilts and fireplace cooking pots. . . .

We go on down, down, down this spiral stairway, nine, ten, yes, it's less than I thought, here's another little door in this platform and it leads to . . . here we are . . . rather like the part we have left, yet completely different in so many ways. . . .

We've come out on the platform about twelve feet above ground, and yet another spiral stairway winds around the tree trunk and ends in the rich green grass of the park. Over in the direction in which we were originally walking is a strangely beautiful building glittering in the sunlight from a thousand mirrorlike facets.

It looks like a palace of green porcelain, only such a sparkling, shining palace, and so beautiful. . . .

Let us walk toward it. The trees are much taller in this park than the one we left—taller, straighter, greener and somehow more elegant. . . .

As we near the palace, we see that it is nearly shrouded in a beautiful rainbow mist, and as we get still nearer, we can see that this is caused by the sunlight playing on the spray from hundreds of beautiful fountains. By contrast with the green, glittering exterior, the interior of the palace is almost dark, but as our eyes become accustomed to the reduced light, we see that this exquisitely ornate building is, indeed, a museum. The cool, greenish room reveals hall upon hall, gallery upon gallery, corridor after corridor, filled with priceless relics of the past. . . .

We start to count the seemingly endless cabinets we pass—seven, eight, nine, ten, eleven, twelve, thirteen, fourteen, fifteen, sixteen, seventeen, eighteen, nineteen, twenty—we are going down deeper and deeper into the earth all the time—thirty-two, thirty-three, thirty-four—and now we are entering a huge chamber in the dimness, a chamber in the great pyramid. . . .

The silence is so complete we can feel it . . . and the lighting is strangely indirect, as if the walls themselves glowed. Although the proportions of the chamber are vast, the richness of the decoration overwhelming, there is something curiously restful here, a quietness so profound that it is soothing, comforting. There's a faint, slightly heady perfume in the air, as of some old, exotic incense . . . we breathe it in. . . .

Sinking onto one of the thronelike chairs, we feel a peaceful drowsiness. . . . Somewhere, there is faint, mysterious music. . . . We feel ourselves falling into a gentle, deliciously enjoyable sleep. . . .

THE AUTOBAHN FANTASY

You're in a car, traveling along an autobahn, and you have been driving for something like three hours. You're just beginning to get tired. . . . During the afternoon, you passed a number of wonderful old castles, like children's fairy castles, some of them, and in all sorts of odd locations, looming high above the trees of the forests, or perched on little islands out in the middle of a lake. . . .

And a little while ago, you saw one that was extraordinarily like a child's fairy castle, made of pink sugar icing, reflecting the late-afternoon sun. . . .

You're thinking about this castle when you suddenly realize that the autobahn is of very poor quality—the road surface seems to be quite rough. Then you realize that instead of being the great six-lane highway that it was, it's now barely two broad tracks getting narrower, and with interlaced tree branches overhead. . . .

Somehow you've lost the autobahn, and now even that track is coming to an end. You haven't even got room to turn around, and it will be impossible to reverse all that way. . . .

You figure you could be near that castle, so you get out of the car and start to walk down the track. . . .

Presently, before you've been walking more than a hundred yards, there's a slight bend in the track and you come across an enormous iron fence. It runs through the woods, and where it intercepts the track there's a pair of great gates. You can see by the flakes on the ground and remains of paint on the surface of the iron that at one time it was gilded. There are the remains of two enormous enamel coats of arms—again, they have suffered the ravages of time—but you can see clearly enough the remains of a double-headed eagle. The gates are open and you go through them and find yourself in what at one time was undoubtedly a beautiful parkland, laid out by someone like Capability Brown, but time has returned it almost to the jungle. . . .

The whole place is running wild. Over to the right, you can see what was once a large and beautiful ornamental pond but is now merely rushes growing thickly round the sides. . . .

Walking on, you see through the trees what seems to be a flight of steps, and your eye moves up, up the fronts of those trees to the tops, and there, peeping over the very tops of those tall trees, you see part of the castle. . . .

So you go on, up the flight of worn stone steps, winding up the hillside, and as you go up and up, you notice something very strange. . . .

First of all, there's a herd of goats grazing at the side of those steps, and they pay no attention to you as you go by. Stranger still, when you've gone a little farther, you come to all kinds of small woodland creatures—field mice, tiny birds, toads—sitting on the steps. You have to pick your way carefully so as not to tread on them, but they ignore you completely, as if you didn't exist. . . .

You make your way on up the steps, and eventually you come to the wall of the castle itself. . . .

Nearby there is a great wooden door, studded with iron. When you get to it, you see that it's slightly ajar. You bang on an enormous knocker, but there's no response, and as you bang harder, the door gives a little, begins to move inward. . . .

Eventually you are able to push the door far enough open to get into the castle. It moves stiffly; a cloud of dust comes down and the hinges squeak. Your heart's already sinking at finding no one there, but now you've become fascinated by the place itself. . . .

You go in and find you are in a great hall, a great stone hall. On the far side of the room, there is an enormous fireplace with a spit big enough to roast a whole ox. On either side of the fireplace, there are recesses in the wall with stone shelves in them, and on either side of those, another opening through which you can see the beginnings of spiral stairways, stone steps running up to the other floors. . . .

In the middle of the room, there's a great old chest. A wooden chest bound with brass. At least you assume that it's brass because its metal clasps and hinges are green with age. You go over and lift the lid and peep inside and it's full of old documents, parchments, written in an unknown tongue. Most of them, though, have maps, and they appear to be maps of the world as it was thought to be in the days prior to Christopher Columbus's exploration.

They are all dusty, and you are about to close the lid when a gleam catches your eye, and in the midst of all those dusty old documents, you can see a bright, gleaming silver goblet. And you pick it out and find inside it a perfectly clean, white, gilt-edged visiting card, blank on both sides. Puzzled, you put it back and close the lid of the chest. But now another gleam catches your eye, and you see, in one of the recesses beside the great fireplace, a lighted candle.

Without thinking who lit it, or why, you realize that the light is fading fast and that the candle will be useful.

You go over and pick it up, and on the spur of the

moment, go into the nearer of the two openings in the wall and start to ascend the spiral stairway. . . .

The stairway is very worn. After a couple of right turns, you come out onto a broad and very long gallery. All down one side there are tall, mullioned windows letting in the light of the setting sun, which falls on the opposite wall, which is covered with rich tapestries. . . .

At intervals, there are great doorways, and beside each door, a suit of armor and all sorts of clothing of different styles and different periods. It's a fascinating gallery. You go inside one of the doors and find yourself in a huge, square bedroom with a vast four-poster bed, some large, clumsy furniture, rather Jacobean in appearance, and an enormous old wardrobe. You peep into the wardrobe, and you find that it's full of the clothes of a bygone age, well-preserved.

Beside the bed, there's a night table. On the table, there's a large, leather-bound volume, and tooled in gilt on the spine is the name *Tolkien.* You open it, thinking it might be *The Hobbit* or *The Lord of the Rings,* but it is Disney's cartoons. You close the book, leave the room and, suddenly filled with the hopelessness of your quest, you decide to go. You make your way back down the corridor to the spiral stairway and down the stairway into the hall, where you find that the lid of the chest is open. You thought you'd closed it. . . . You go and look at it for a moment, and then close it again. As you go up toward the candle, it immediately goes out. You're left alone in the darkness. . . .

You make your way to the door rather rapidly. As you descend those worn stone steps, the little animals are still there; they still ignore your presence. Further down, the herd of goats is still there; they still ignore your presence. And when you get to the foot of the stairway, it's getting quite dark, and there's a thick mist arising from that mere, but you can see where the gates are, and when you get to the gates you can see the car. . . .

It is where you left it, but not how you left it. When you get closer to it, you find it's not jammed in a little track but in a rest area at the side of the autobahn!

You get in and drive away. Ahead you can see the lights of your destination. Only a few kilometers to go, and after a while, you can't be sure whether you really visited that castle, or whether it was a daydream.

A MEDITATION ON THE SEA
(Jules Cashford)

You are walking along the edge of the sea, your feet burning from the hot sand. The sea is bluer than you have ever known it, motionless and quite transparent, and as you look down into it, you seem to see the sky moving in the sea and the sea swaying to the movement of the sky.

You look up and in the distance, a fine mist glistens with the colors of heat and silence. The air shimmers toward you and through you, dissolving your body in waves of light. Only the gulls make shapes of the silence, tilting and gliding on invisible tides—but then they slowly slide off into the mist until they are nothing but faint curves of white, and then these, too, disappear. Your breath floats out after them into mist, and you, following your breath, find that you are now in the sea yourself. You are floating gently on your back, drawn also toward the mist, coming ever closer and closer, and as you feel the soft sprinkling on your face, the mist vanishes so suddenly that it might never have been there.

A radiant light surrounds you, and now you no longer know whether you are floating in the sea or in the sky, and it no longer matters. They have become one blue circle around you, and you are poised in the center, suspended in a blue void.

From far away, from a dream deep within you, a feeling is coming toward you; it has no name, no image; it is just a feeling. It is not like any feeling you have ever had; it is new, absolutely itself. You don't know what it is; you know only that it is coming, that it is here. You don't try to experience it; you let it come first; you let *it* feel *you.* This feeling will lead you back to where you are, back to the circle of sea and sky. You are the feeling of being here now in this new way, poised between sea and sky. You and the feeling are one.

In this new way of feeling, you begin to swim effortlessly back toward the shore, and you become aware that your body never moved through the water quite this way before. You were never so still, yet still moving.

Now you are coming to the sea's end and the land's call and, suddenly, *you* are the sound of the surf's fall and breaking . . . and the pebbles pulled back under and tossed forward . . . and the sand-feet which wrinkle and curl . . . and the flat weight of the earth which rises up through your body and stands you on this shore . . . where you are now. Your eyes open to the sparkling dance of the sun, the sea, and the limitless sky.

A JOURNEY OUT OF THE BODY
(Nona Coxhead)

You have been on vacation in another country, and now you are coming home by plane. You have been hurrying, going through all the hustle and bustle of carrying luggage, showing tickets and passport, and now you have settled into a seat by the window and are beginning to relax. You are a little afraid of flying, so you try to make yourself as calm as possible, as you would in meditation . . .

Soon, you feel very quiet and centered in yourself, and

when the plane takes off, leaves the runway and begins to ascend, you feel no fear, but a quiet exhilaration, a sense of being lifted upward in yourself as well as by the plane . . .

You look out the window and note that the wet, misty morning is quickly vanishing, being replaced by the white brightness of fleecy clouds. Gradually, the last trace of land disappears and the clouds become one solid mass ablaze with sunlight. It is like another world, and you feel that the clouds must be substantial, that you could walk on them. They are very pleasing, and you wish it were so, that you could actually leave the plane and move about on the clouds . . .

But you know it is an illusion, and you sit back and go into a doze . . . Time passes. You sleep a while.

Waking, but still very relaxed and calm, you wonder what has happened to your fear of being so high up above, so disconnected with firm ground. You feel a sense of freedom now, freedom from the confinement of earth and a particular limitation of movement. You close your eyes and feel the movement of the plane, seem to merge with it. You are going along through space with the same speed as the plane . . .

A sensation of lightness fills you, a feeling of floating quite free of the plane, of being able to fly separately and apart from the plane . . .

You feel yourself leave your physical body sitting there in the plane seat, and you float quite easily through the plane body, outside the window, start traveling along with the plane, floating and free . . .

It is such a joyous feeling, so beautiful and free, that you start playing with the possibilities, whirling and spinning and looping gently and easily about the plane . . . You look in the windows as you float and fly and see the faces of passengers inside. You wonder how it can be that they are not aware of you, or aware that they, too, could be out here flying . . .

You feel the soft, billowing clouds pass gently over you, and you wave your arms through the brilliant, transparent stuff, enjoying the invisible yet real texture of this shaped air . . .

You find airwaves to ride on, like dips in scenic railways, with the same thrill, and up, up, up you go into stronger and stronger light, into a great golden aura of warm light, and you see the plane far below like a glinting beetle scurrying through a cloud landscape . . .

Now you float gently downward again, filled with a joyful sense of a limitless universe in which you are really free, can always, if you want to, detach yourself from your physical body and take off into space . . .

You are happy now to return to that body, to the plane, and the old familiar confinement, so you gently descend, rolling, spiraling downward so as to imbibe the full feeling of grace, ease, agility of your bodiless self. And then, with the gentlest of transitions, by just thinking of it, you are back in your seat.

The people sitting next to you have no idea where you have been. It is your secret. You feel exhilarated, yet at peace. Soon, now, you are aware that the clouds beneath you are breaking up, dispersing . . . Glimpsed in between them now are miniature shapes of land mass in sepia browns and soft greens, with small, glinting strands that gradually turn out to be rivers, and little odd-shaped gems that turn out to be lakes . . .

Soon, the land is familiar to you. Huddled designs of toy houses turn out to be farms, settlements, villages, towns. Buildings emerge from geometric patterns against the earth; thousands of scurrying ants are revealed as cars and trucks; and the little moving dots that scattered the landscape are people.

They become recognizable as different kinds of people . . .

There are other planes like this one . . . You are brought down from the great heights to the hard ground of your familiar planet . . . It is the airport, and you are home. But somehow, you will never be quite the same person you were when you left; in you is the secret feeling of having been away, not only from home, but from the limitation of your physical self.

THE BLOWHOLE
(A Meditation for the Release of
Self-concealed Experience)
(C. Maxwell Cade)

There are no thoughts in your mind, neither words nor images. You are relaxed and comfortable; all is restful and peaceful. Now you are aware of something dimly beginning to form within your mind, like the memory of a dream. Slowly, gradually, the picture begins to clear. You are in a train, just pulling into what appears to be a large railway station. There are many people waiting on the platforms, and many more at the restaurant, shops and stands. There is a happy, holiday sort of air about everything.

The train comes to a stop and the people crowded in the corridor begin to get out. You look around for your luggage, but there isn't any. You seem vaguely to remember that this is only a day trip, so you get out, still with an uncomfortable feeling of having forgotten something. When you get to the barrier, you find you have the ticket in your hand. The interior of the station is brightly lit by daylight passing through the glass roof, and outside, the streets are bathed in brilliant sunlight, but between the two you have to pass through the gloom of vast stone archways. From immediately outside the station, you have a view over the town to the sea and the long pier, and over to the west, the white chalk of cliffs and the green of the golf course.

As you descend the first steep part of the hill, the view disappears behind the houses. Then, for a while, even the direct sunlight is cut off as you walk through the narrow alleyways of the old market quarter. Presently you come out of the built-up area onto the broad lawns and pathways which adjoin the beach. Despite the strong breeze off the sea, the hot sunlight bites into you.

Still with the slightly dazed feeling that you must have fallen asleep on the train, you are looking around for some clue as to where you should be going when your attention is gripped by an enormous poster. There is an artist's impression of a great wave breaking upon a cliff, at the foot of which there is an opening like a cave. From the back of the cliff, a gigantic waterspout rises high into the air, watched by a fascinated crowd of people, seemingly packed onto the many balconies of a tall skyscraper. A vivid red arrow points along the promenade to the West, and beneath the arrow in vivid, wavy lettering is the legend: THE EIGHTH WONDER OF THE WORLD! NOTHING LIKE IT ANYWHERE ELSE ON EARTH! VISIT THE BLOWHOLE! There follows a rather lurid description of this natural phenomenon, which apparently occurs once at every high tide, and is supported by other attractions such as restaurants, an aquarium, botanical gardens, supermarket and theater. Even these advertising excesses cannot dispel the sense of wonderment aroused by the artist's representation, and when your eye falls upon the panel which announces TODAY'S BLOWHOLE TIMES and you see that you have just forty minutes to get there, you head for the little station plainly labeled "Blowhole Railway."

As the comfortable miniature train carries you the two miles to your destination, you are fascinated by the change in the landscape. The formal promenade soon gives way to downs and chalk cliffs, which in turn yield place to even higher faces of jagged rock. The train deposits you at another little station near the foot of the high cliffs, and a moving platform carries you deep into the rock to where the elevators are. The transformation from the barren and rather threatening rocks at the foot of the cliffs to what awaits you at the top is remarkable. You step out of the elevator into a vast, bustling, ultramodern building; your first impression is that it is the departure lounge of the World's largest airport. Through high glass windows on one side, you can see the beautiful botanical gardens; nearby, a neon sign announces: "Escalator to Aquarium"; further off are the movie theaters offering four different programs and one of the numerous restaurants. More than two hundred yards away, a multiple escalator rises high up toward a brilliant electric sign which says "Supermarket." Everywhere there are crowds of eager sightseers, smartly uniformed staff, boutiques, stands, little shops and automats.

Suddenly, a bell-like tone comes over the loudspeaker system, followed by a pleasant female voice saying: "This morning's Bore will commence in fifteen minutes' time. Visitors wishing to see the waterspout should obtain their tickets and go to Exit Four immediately." The announcement is repeated in French, German and Spanish. A few minutes later, you are one of several hundred people standing at the railing of an enormous balcony overlooking a great natural basin in the rock. Over the loudspeaker system a quiet, authoritative voice tells you what to expect, where to look for it, and gives a brief explanation of tidal bores and blowholes. The voice ceases rather abruptly as the sound engineers switch over to microphones in the rock face more than a mile away, and the frightening roar of the tidal bore presses on your eardrums. At the far side of the rock basin, the water bubbles and heaves; waves begin in a series of concentric circles, but soon lose their regularity and become wildly disordered, more and more violent, and then erupt into a gigantic spout which rises hundreds of feet into the air. Instinctively, you look around to see if your position is secure. The other watchers are showing similar uneasiness. The water spout grows even higher, a cataclysmic deluge. Although the point of emergence of the water is eight or nine hundred yards away, spray begins to obscure the glass shield in front of your balcony.

As you watch, a peculiar change takes place in your consciousness. You are no longer watching something taking place *out there,* but something taking place *in here,* within yourself. The roaring, twisting, boiling torrent is not something which is manifesting cold water a few hundred yards away. It is something real, alive, and darkly unpleasant . . . from somewhere deep in memory, perhaps from childhood . . . now surfacing . . . emerging . . .

No longer aware of the crowds, the balconies, the rock basin, you are only aware of this pounding, whirling turmoil, this mysterious, compelling unhappiness . . .

Then, as you experience it, you also begin to watch it; you see it become something impersonal, not as something that happened to you yourself, but to someone you knew in the past. And now you stand apart from it and know that it was something not so terrible at all but something that was part of life, that had to be that way, that only happened as it should. You look back upon the whole incident which caused you so much suffering and see it as if through some magic lens, becoming smaller and smaller, dwindling away, vanishing . . .

Your attention moves off now to the dance of morning mist as it billows and flows in silent arabesques. The mist softens and begins to dissolve in the warm caress of sunlight. With the disappearance of the mist, you find yourself walking in a woodland glade. You reach out and touch the wrinkled bark of an old oak. Suddenly all is clear, all is bright, just as everything around you is clear and bright, touched by the glow of morning sun. You can remember the dream of the blowhole, and the incident from your past. But they are just dreams—only old dreams. And to-day's sunshine is so real!

Walk on through the sparkle of spring sunshine, the budding, blowing beauty of new life all around you. And know that it will always be like this.

Sensory Sequences

1. VISUAL.

Imagine all the colors in a child's box of paints or crayons—pink, ultramarine, orange, yellow, mauve, pur-ple, brown, black, white, dark green, light green, gam-boge, crimson.

Watch a comic cartoon in the movies or on TV.

In your imagination, ride through familiar streets, too fast to be able to see faces clearly.

In a darkened room, gaze at the fire, which may be gas, electric or preferably a real old-fashioned log fire.

From the top of the Post Office Tower, Empire State Building or from a landing airplane, see antlike people in the streets.

The stars on a clear summer's night . . . sunset.

2. TACTILE.

Imagine the feel of your own body as you wash under a hot shower.

Snowballs, cold enough to numb your fingers, and the winter wind nipping your ears.

An egg breaks in your hand—feel the stickiness of it.

Brushing your teeth . . . tying shoelaces . . . buttoning a coat . . . combing your hair.

The prickliness of a pineapple.

3. SOUND.

The ringing of happy church bells.

A street-musician's violin.

The roar of a subway train.

A parrot or myna bird, crying "Hello, good morning."

A grandfather clock, slowly ticking in a quiet room.

Midnight on New Year's Eve—crowds singing "Auld Lang Syne."

The lowing of cows and the bleating of sheep.

On a train journey, the sound of the wheels on the rails and the roar as it passes under a bridge.

The fearful sound of ambulance sirens and fire engines.

An orchestra playing sentimental tunes.

The news on radio or TV.

4. SMELL AND TASTE.

Christmas dinner—think about it carefully, see it vividly.

Honey, bananas, fireworks.

Gas and diesel fumes in a traffic jam.

The perfume department in a large store.

Shoe polish. Soap. Toothpaste.

5. KINESTHESIA

Imagine yourself on a swing.

Walking home with heavy shopping bags, and the rain dripping down your neck.

At a massage clinic or sauna bath . . . an easy, soothing massage.

Playing golf, hockey or football.

A brisk cliff-top walk on a perfect day.

At a fairground, riding on bumper cars or a ferris wheel.

Straining to undo a tight screw cap or water tap.

Dancing, modern or ballroom.

Vigorous physical jerks.

Sunbathing, or just lazing on a sheltered, deserted beach.

Schultz Autogenic Relaxation Sequences

Lie quietly in a comfortable position with arms and legs uncrossed. Repeat and execute the following, slowly:

I take a slow, deep breath.

I hold my breath, then breathe out slowly.

I take another slow, deep breath.

I hold my breath and pull my toes up toward my head, tightening my calf and leg muscles.

I feel the tension.

I breathe out and relax completely.

I take another slow, deep breath.

I hold my breath and bite down as hard as I can, tightening my jaw muscles.

I feel the tension.

I breathe out and relax completely.

I take another slow, deep breath.

I hold my breath and make a fist with both hands, tightening my arm and shoulder muscles.

I feel the tension.

I breathe out and relax completely.

I take another slow, deep breath.

I hold my breath while tightening my stomach and neck muscles.

I feel the tension.

I breathe out and let my muscles go limp.

I take another slow, deep breath.

I hold my breath and tighten every muscle in my body until I feel my body start to tremble with tension.

I breathe out and let go completely.

I take another slow, deep breath.

I hold my breath and tighten every muscle in my body.

I breathe out and relax completely.

I take another slow, deep breath.

I hold my breath and tighten every muscle in my body.

I hold the tension.

I breathe out and relax completely.

Throughout the rest of this exercise, I concentrate on slow, deep breathing.

I am beginning to feel calm and quiet . . .

I am beginning to feel comfortable and quiet . . .

I am beginning to feel quite relaxed . . .

My feet feel heavy and relaxed.

My feet feel heavy and relaxed.

My ankles feel heavy and relaxed.

My ankles feel heavy and relaxed.

My calves feel heavy and relaxed.

My calves feel heavy and relaxed.

My knees feel heavy and relaxed.

My knees feel heavy and relaxed.

My thighs feel heavy and relaxed.

My thighs feel heavy and relaxed.

My hips feel heavy and relaxed.

My hips feel heavy and relaxed.

The whole of my legs feel heavy and relaxed.

The whole of my legs feel heavy and relaxed.

My hands feel heavy and relaxed.

My hands feel heavy and relaxed.

My arms feel heavy and relaxed.

My arms feel heavy and relaxed.

My shoulders feel heavy and relaxed.

My shoulders feel heavy and relaxed.

My hands, my arms and my shoulders all feel heavy and relaxed.

My hands, my arms and my shoulders all feel heavy and relaxed.

My neck feels heavy and relaxed.

My neck feels heavy and relaxed.

My jaws feel heavy and relaxed.

My jaws feel heavy and relaxed.

My forehead feels heavy and relaxed.

My forehead feels heavy and relaxed.

My neck, my jaws and my forehead all feel heavy and relaxed.

My neck, my jaws and my forehead all feel heavy and relaxed.

My whole body feels heavy and relaxed.

My whole body feels heavy and relaxed.

My breathing is getting deeper and deeper.

My breathing is getting deeper and deeper.

I can feel the sun shining down on me, warming the top of my head.

I can feel the sun shining down on me, warming the top of my head.

The top of my head feels heavy and warm.

The top of my head feels heavy and warm.

The relaxing warmth flows into my right shoulder.

My right shoulder feels heavy and warm.

My right shoulder feels heavy and warm.

The relaxing warmth flows down to my right hand.

My right hand feels heavy and warm.

My right hand feels heavy and warm.

The relaxing warmth flows back up my right arm.

My right arm feels heavy and warm.

My right arm feels heavy and warm.

The relaxing warmth flows up through my right elbow into my right shoulder.

My right elbow, my right shoulder, feel heavy and warm.

My right elbow, my right shoulder, feel heavy and warm.

My breathing is getting deeper and deeper.

My breathing is getting deeper and deeper.

The relaxing warmth flows slowly throughout the whole of my back.

I can feel the warmth relaxing my back.

My back feels heavy and warm.

My back feels heavy and warm.

The relaxing warmth flows up my back and into my neck.

My neck feels heavy and warm.

My neck feels heavy and warm.

The relaxing warmth flows into my left shoulder.

My left shoulder feels heavy and warm.

My left shoulder feels heavy and warm.

The relaxing warmth flows down to my left hand.

My left hand feels heavy and warm.

My left hand feels heavy and warm.

The relaxing warmth flows back up my left arm.

My left arm feels heavy and warm.

My left arm feels heavy and warm.

The relaxing warmth flows up through my left elbow into
my left shoulder.

My left elbow, my left shoulder, feel heavy and warm.

My left elbow, my left shoulder, feel heavy and warm.

The relaxing warmth flows into my heart.

My heart feels warm and easy.

My heart feels warm and easy.

My heartbeat is calm and regular.

My heartbeat is calm and regular.

The relaxing warmth flows down into my stomach.

My stomach feels warm and quiet.

My stomach feels warm and quiet.

My breathing is getting even deeper.

My breathing is getting even deeper.

The relaxing warmth flows down into my right thigh.

My right thigh feels heavy and warm.

My right thigh feels heavy and warm.

The relaxing warmth flows down into my right foot.

My right foot feels heavy and warm.

My right foot feels heavy and warm.

The relaxing warmth flows slowly up through my right calf, to my right knee, to my right thigh.

The whole of my right leg feels heavy and warm.

The whole of my right leg feels heavy and warm.

The relaxing warmth flows down into my left thigh.

My left thigh feels heavy and warm.

My left thigh feels heavy and warm.

The relaxing warmth flows down into my left foot.

My left foot feels heavy and warm.

My left foot feels heavy and warm.

The relaxing warmth flows slowly up through my left calf, to my left knee, to my left thigh.

The whole of my left leg feels heavy and warm.

The whole of my left leg feels heavy and warm.

My breathing is getting deeper and deeper.

My breathing is getting deeper and deeper.

The relaxing warmth flows up through my abdomen, through my stomach and into my heart.

My heart feels warm and easy.

My heart feels warm and easy.

My heartbeat is calm and regular.

My heartbeat is calm and regular.

My heart pumps relaxing warmth throughout my entire body.

My whole body is heavy, warm, relaxed.

My whole body is heavy, warm, relaxed.

My whole body feels very quiet and very serene.

My whole body feels very comfortable, and very relaxed.

My mind is still. My mind is quiet. My mind is easy.

I withdraw my thoughts from my surroundings.

I withdraw my thoughts from the environment.

Nothing exists around me.

I feel serene, secure, still.

My thoughts are all turned inward.

I am at ease, completely at ease.

Deep within my mind, I can visualize and experience myself as relaxed.

I am comfortable and still.

My mind is quiet and still.

I feel a new sense of well-being.

I am breathing more and more deeply.

I am breathing more and more deeply.

My body and mind are in perfect harmony.

As I prepare to return to my normal level of awareness, I will bring with me all the comfort and relaxation I have created at these deeper levels of concentration.

I take a deep, pleasant breath, slowly open my eyes and stretch all the muscles in my body, filling myself with new energy.

Chapter 3

The Art of Meditation
As It Relates
to Biofeedback

Most people today are aware of the tremendous upsurge of interest in the ancient practice of meditation. From the Westerner's point of view, interest in the practice has been greatly spurred by scientific monitoring, which has provided it with a sound physiological basis. Both Eastern and Western methods lead to a state of deep relaxation, and in the West, this effect has recently become known as the relaxation response (technically, the trophotrophic response).

In order to understand the subsequent developments of our higher levels of awareness, one must look at the point from which they expanded.

First described by Walter Hess in 1957, the relaxation response is the very opposite of the fight-or-flight response of stress. The physiological correlates have been shown to include:

1. decrease in oxygen consumption

2. reduction in carbon dioxide elimination

3. reduction in: (a)   heart rate
                      (b)   respiratory rate
                      (c)   blood pressure
                      (d)   blood lactate
                      (e)   muscle tone
                      (f)   blood cortisone levels

4. increase in perfusion of internal organs

5. increase in finger temperature

6. increase in apparent basal skin resistance, which can be used as an accurate measure of the extent of relaxation

In addition, there are accompanying changes in the pattern of brain electrical activity: the EEG shows an increase in the intensity of slow alpha waves and occasional theta-wave activity during meditation, while muscle tonus, as measured by the myograph, decreases. All these changes are consistent with a generalized decrease in the activity of the sympathetic nervous system, and they are distinctly different from the physiological changes observed when sitting quietly or in sleep.

It was the observation of these profound differences between sleep, resting and meditation that led Dr. Keith Wallace and his colleagues at Harvard Medical School, in 1971, to describe meditation as "an alert, hypometabolic state" constituting a "fourth major state of consciousness."

Without special training, subjective experience is no guide to one's physiological state during any altered state of consciousness. For this reason, if one is learning to meditate primarily or largely in order to gain the health benefits, it is helpful to employ some instrumental indication of the depth of the relaxation response. One's self-awareness increases so rapidly that the instruments can soon be discarded.

At this level, which is not concerned with the alleged spiritual or mental benefits of meditation but with the basic physical and mental benefits of the relaxation response, meditation is considered only as an altered state of consciousness (ASC) which is accompanied by a deeper state of rest than occurs in sleep, and which also provides the opportunity for us to avail ourselves of our hitherto unmanifested creativity by facilitating the transmission of dreamlike imagery from the right to the left hemisphere of the brain.

How, then, can one elicit at will this beneficial relaxation response? According to Dr. Herbert Benson, four basic elements are usually required:

1. A Mental Device: there should be a verbal or visual relaxation technique to shift the subject's mind from logical, externally oriented thought to the internally oriented imaging or intuitive mental activity of the altered state of consciousness which accompanies the relaxation response.

2. A Passive Attitude: if distracting thoughts do occur during the sense-awareness exercises and other devices of the relaxation training, they should be disregarded and one's attention should be redirected to the technique. One should never worry about how well one is performing the technique. Worry is an arousing activity which destroys the relaxation response by producing the fight-or-flight response instead.

3. Decreased Muscle Tonus: the subject should be in a reasonably comfortable posture so that minimum muscular work is needed. Nevertheless, too much comfort is to be avoided, since this is more likely to induce sleep than meditation.

4. A Quiet Environment: for the beginner, a quiet environment with decreased environmental stimuli is usually chosen. Most techniques instruct the beginner

to close his eyes. However, once again, although quietness may assist the beginner, the object of the training is to achieve calmness and relaxation at will, no matter what the environmental conditions may be.

Because of the now-established physiological benefits of the relaxation response, many psychosomatic ailments, which are mainly related to states of overarousal, can be greatly improved or even completely cured within a few weeks of regular practice. Anxiety, strain, tension and aggressiveness all decrease, while there is an increase in self-control and an improvement in general health and energy. What is more, as one gets to know oneself much better than before, one can head off stress before it has a chance to affect the nervous system.

That is why, in our biofeedback training, we begin with the relaxation response and with the heavy initial emphasis on EEG techniques and monitoring, together with the visual and/or sensory sequences, to achieve the deepest possible relaxation of both body and mind. The principal reason for this is that previous to the training, our students may not have achieved even rudimentary self-awareness. We find that most beginners have previously spent long stretches of time going about their daily lives with little but exterior, or environmental, awareness; that they have passed through their waking hours transferring their attention to this place or that activity with such minimal inner awareness that it was highly unlikely that they would be able to open up their (left hemisphere) consciousness to the contents (including body awareness) of their right hemisphere without a great deal of instrument-assisted training. Nevertheless, the great majority of students find their increased awareness so rewarding that, within a few months, they have learned a high degree of self-control of internal states without being dependent on the machines.

For beginners in biofeedback training, and for people generally, it is very difficult to grasp the concept that our so-called normal waking state is neither the highest nor the most effective state of which the human mind is capable, that there are other states of vastly greater awareness which one can enter briefly and then return to normal living enriched, enlivened and enhanced.

The main goal for biofeedback trainees, therefore, is to gain conviction through firsthand experience of the effects of their own other-than-normal states while being monitored by the machines.

Our methods for assisting in this cooperative procedure generally begin with a quietly intoned suggestion for relaxation, followed by a guided imagery sequence to induce mental concentration and fluency.

We ask the subjects, who are connected to their EEG and ESR monitors, to sit upright and in a comfortable position, though with spines straight (this seems of particular importance in achieving the balance of relaxation and alertness that stops short of sleep). Then, slowly and quietly, the instructor or researcher intones the following relaxation sequence (based on a technique of Ainslie Meares, an Australian psychoanalyst), which can be read aloud or put on tape, though it is quite easy to memorize:

Relaxed, relaxed, relaxed.
The whole of my body relaxed.
Relaxed and calm.
Calmness all through me.
Calmness in my face, calmness in my mind.

Relaxed, relaxed, relaxed.

My legs, arms, whole body relaxed.

It is in my face.

The muscles around my eyes are relaxed, the muscles
around my mouth.

My lips, tongue and throat—all deeply relaxed.

My whole face smooths out.

My forehead is relaxed, deeply relaxed and smooth—no
furrows in it.

I feel it in my mind.

Relaxed, relaxed, relaxed.

It is natural to relax. It is nature's way.

To rest, to relax, and to be calm.

It is Nature's way to renew strength,

Strength of body and calmness of mind.

I feel the relaxation and the calmness all through me.

Relaxed, relaxed, relaxed.

I feel the relaxation. I feel my muscles let go.

They let go all through me.

In my limbs, my torso, my neck and shoulders.

Deeper and deeper relaxation—it is in my mind.

I let go, I let go, I let go.

Relaxed, relaxed, relaxed.

Utterly calm and relaxed.

Nothing disturbs me. Nothing alarms me,

I am more and more at peace.

I feel the relaxation and the ease.

The ease of it all through me.

The ease of it in my face, in my mind, in my easy breathing.

Breathing easily and deeply, easily and deeply, easily and deeply.

And now, at this point, the instructor continues on into the chosen sequence, which may be any one of a large variety of sense experiences, according to which aspect of awareness training we need to emphasize or the stage of advancement of the subjects.

Given here are a few contrasting sequences, concluding with a series of very short word pictures closely strung together, switching from one theme to another without pause. This is in order to circumvent subjects becoming accustomed to one theme and perhaps losing concentration and therefore relaxation depth, and also because it is a way of intensifying the depth to a more profound trance state.

Five Word Pictures with Contrasting Themes

1. You are standing at the end of a pier on a sunny but windy day. Be aware of the light spray falling upon you and of the thumping of the waves against the supports of the pier; of the fishy salt tang on the air; see the regatta, and the sea dotted with the brightly colored sails of the competitive sailing craft. See the sparkle of the sun on the waves, and hear the harsh cry of the sea gulls.

2. Now we change the picture: you're out in the garden on a clear winter's night, thousands upon thousands of stars are twinkling against a velvety black sky. There is a

scent of burning leaves and twigs from a nearby bonfire
. . . the wind is cold but not strong. Against the sky to the
south, there is silhouetted an old church spire from where
you can hear an owl calling. From behind the horizon,
flickering light plays in the sky, and faintly you can hear
the roll of thunder.

3. Now you are on a high hill crowned with a small wood
of very ancient trees. The day is peaceful and serene, the
sky a deep unbroken blue. The fields below are bathed in
sunshine, making a patchwork quilt of green and brown
and gold. All around where you are standing, bluebells
grow in profusion. Over to your right, a long viaduct
crosses a double bend in the river. You see and hear
faintly a train passing over the viaduct. You hear clearly
the lowing of cows from an unseen pasture.

4. Now it is night and you are at a fairground. Try to picture the scene: you watch the great wheel going round
and round, the merry-go-round, the tunnel of love, the
switchback railway, the haunted house, the bumper cars,
all brightly illuminated with many-colored lights. Waves of
deafening music, a babel of voices, the cries of the bark-
ers: "roll up, roll up, roll up." The oily smells from food
stalls, the odor of burned gunpowder from the rifle range.
And it is raining; not heavily, just a drizzle, but enough so
that you cannot ignore it.

5. Now visualize a bay with the tide far, far out . . . and a
vast, flat space of sand between land and sea; the golden
sand is rippled by the tides, scattered with shells and sea-
weed and little pools which reflect the sky. Far off, the
green, white-capped waves are breaking on the beach,
and the wild calls of sea birds fill the air with strange
music. A sky of restful opal and mother-of-pearl encloses
the bay . . .

These sequences are often given alternate endings in order to emphasize or bring out some particular character revelation, to challenge some aspect of individual self-awareness or simply to increase subjects' awareness of some hidden problem or reluctance. Also the sensory exploration can be so directed or elaborated as to supply additional facets of self-awareness.

One of the main objectives is to become aware of what overarouses or causes cessation of the alpha signal. One student, for instance, found her alpha suddenly blocked and her meter swinging to high arousal because of a very deeply felt disagreement with the philosophy of what the instructor was saying; the moment the subject intellectualized, her state of calm tranquillity ceased. This gives a rough idea of how frequently the nervous system is bombarded with arousal states in the round of daily life. This student was immediately able to revive her calm and her alpha signal because she had learned how to do so. Not only had she observed the physiological effect of mental disturbance, but she was able to pinpoint a source of stress of which she had been unaware. She could now hope to control puzzling psychosomatic symptoms by becoming aware of her tendency to bring unnecessary stress into daily life and so to learn to become more detached and relaxed.

At the end of these sessions, the subjects are brought back to their ordinary state. Their instruments have been monitored and records made of their relaxation depths. They are told what they achieved instrumentally, and they are asked for their subjective reactions to the sequences. In this way, relaxation-response training and expansion of self-awareness soon become synonymous.

So far, we have dealt with the relaxation response without connotations of meditation as an art in itself: we have considered and applied only the physiological aspects of the deep relaxation accompanying sitting very still, quieting the mind and developing the imagination through sensory and visual sequences. What we still want to discuss is meditation in relation to the instruments of biofeedback monitoring, leaving the many techniques of meditation without machines as an advance into higher levels of awareness when the learned physiological states have become ingrained and unforgettable. In this way, there is no question that subjects are merely daydreaming, musing or wasting time and effort to achieve a state that doesn't live up to its reputation, provides none of the claimed benefits and is an effort without reward, often causing the very strain it is so widely maintained as dispelling.

For, in applying our instruments to some people who have practiced Eastern forms of meditation for a long time, we found an unexpected and astonishing fact: several of them were not in the appropriate depths of alpha-theta associated with instrumented meditation. They were achieving no more or less alpha (plus beta) than any untrained person who sits extremely still with eyes closed. They were as surprised as we were, but even more so when we gave them some training: they were unanimous in recognizing the difference in the immediate expansion and deepening of consciousness.

They could not have explained it to anyone who had not had the experience of proper meditation, but it was a revelation that many persons who believe, or want to believe, they are meditating are only bordering on its edges. It also explains why so many give up on or belittle the value of meditation. If one is not meditating correctly, the only advantage of assuming its posture and stillness is the tranquilizing effect of any restful procedure. The disadvantages (and sometimes dangers) are in the strain and effort, the forced containment of restlessness, the frustration of falling short of what is often described as a state of bliss, and disappointment in what, for many thousands of people, is the last hope for a new and better way of life.

Eastern masters of the discipline have long known of these difficulties. If every aspiring meditator were meditating correctly, the famous state of enlightenment would be common, indeed widespread, not rare; there would be more gurus (teachers) than students!

The "anatomy" of meditation, therefore, is what we deal with here, the basic concepts and practice that are the mental side of the mind-body coin.

Let us start with what meditation is *not*. We must be very clear that it is not concentration. Concentration comes before meditation—a long way before and a long way below. It is enormously important that we should understand the distinction between the absolutely essential mental-development exercises which precede true meditation and meditation itself.

As Krishnamurti, the Indian philosopher, says: "In its beginning, meditation is an exercise in control of attention. . . . Attention has no border, no frontier to cross; attention is clarity, clear of all thought. Thought is the cessation of meditation; good meditation begins with the cessation of thought. Awareness of this is to be attentive. . . . Meditation is not an intellectual process, which is still within the area of thought. Meditation is the freedom from thought. . . ."

Learning to control one's attention is, therefore, as Patanjali stated so clearly 2300 years ago, the basis of all meditation, and meditative exercises may roughly be divided into two kinds, concentrative meditation and mindfulness, according to how the attention is focused.

In concentrative meditation (on which most Christian, Sufi and Yoga techniques are based), one gives one's whole, undivided attention to a single unchanging or repeated perception or idea. The aim of this procedure is to reach a state of undeviating absorption in the object of one's meditation, so that one has excluded awareness of all competing stimuli. This is one of the oldest kinds of meditation and in many cases overlaps with the techniques used to attain ecstasy (such as drumbeats, whirling, chanting and the use of hallucinogens like mescaline).

Mindfulness, on the other hand, is the art of giving one's whole attention to the changing content of one's awareness (or a particular part of one's total awareness) without choosing the contents and without clinging to a particular content once another intrudes upon it. The aim is to become fully aware of *everything* of which one is aware.

To learn to still the everyday mind, to stop the flow of idle chatter, the internal record player that perpetually exhorts, discusses, questions and lectures, and the remorseless voice that rolls on with ceaseless recriminations, rehearsals, puns, alliterations and even snatches of poetry and popular song, is the fundamental lesson of meditation.

That this needs patience, persistence and a kind of trustful letting-go of one's attachment to "normal" reality, which for all its faults is at least familiar, cannot be denied. Initially, one is apt to cling to personal identity in the fear of something happening to it in this altered state, in the same way that death is feared because one does not know what it is. People without these fears and reluctances usually begin to meditate with greater ease.

But our attention is generally deployed outward for good reason. It would certainly be difficult for us to behave in an appropriate and self-preservative manner if we were continuously paying attention to every single internal process. We ignore these inner signals in favor of those coming from the external environment, which may require immediate action related to survival.

Meditating, then, at this stage, is a deliberate switching-off of these external stimuli that prepare the nervous system for fight or flight, and a courting of the heretofore unconscious stimuli which have hitherto been reduced to a minimum by the process of individual selective awareness.

The practice of meditation has many extraordinarily different forms. The distinction between those forms with a central idea and those without one is only one of contrasting interpretations. Some techniques emphasize mental imagery, others discourage images in case they be mistaken for reality; some use real visual forms, concentrating upon a lamp, a vase or a mandala (religious symbol), while others stress complete withdrawal from the senses. Some call for absolute inactivity on the part of the meditator, while others employ movements of the fingers, arms or whole body, walking, dancing or whirling (as with the Dervishes). Many forms are based upon more or less complex breathing rituals.

In our own biofeedback training, we give special importance to the forms based upon awareness of diaphragmatic breathing. As a mindful exercise, it helps to gradually reduce the gap between conscious and unconscious control. As Dr. Walpola Rahula has said in his book *What the Buddha Taught*:

> You breathe in and out all day and night, but you are never mindful of it, you never for a second concentrate your mind on it. Now you are going to do just this. Breathe in and out as usual, without any effort or strain. Now, bring your mind to concentrate on your breathing-in and breathing-out; let your mind watch and observe your breathing in and out. When you breathe, you sometimes take deep breaths, sometimes not. This does not matter at all. Breathe normally and naturally. The only thing is that when you take deep breaths you should be aware that they are deep breaths. . . .

In other words, *your mind should be so fully concentrated on your breathing that you are aware of its movements and changes. Forget all other things—your surroundings, your environment; do not raise your eyes to look at anything.* Try to do this for five or ten minutes.

At the beginning, you will find it extremely difficult to control your mind to concentrate on your breathing. You will be astonished how your mind runs away. But if you continue to practice this exercise twice daily, you will gradually, little by little, begin to be able to concentrate your mind on your breathing.

After a certain period, you will experience just that split second when your mind is fully concentrated on your breathing when you will not hear even sounds nearby—when no external world exists for you. This slight moment is such a tremendous experience for you, full of joy, happiness and tranquility, that you would like to continue it. But still you cannot. Yet if you go on practicing this regularly, you may repeat the experience again and again for longer and longer periods. That is the moment when you lose yourself in your mindfulness of breathing. *As long as you are conscious of yourself, you can never concentrate on anything.* This exercise of mindfulness of breathing is meant to develop concentration leading up to very high mystic attainments.

The development of mindfulness may not come quickly, but eventually, during meditation, the specific focus of attention imperceptibly narrows down to the awareness of the inner communication with the muscle activity controlling the diaphragm. Control is not consciously exercised but is rather observed.

The vast number of psychophysiological experiments carried out in recent years in connection with biofeedback and the voluntary control of internal states has shown that, provided the attention can be focused unwaveringly for a sufficient length of time (which depends on the individual's psychological type), the self-consciousness tends to identify with the focus of attention. Therefore, self-consciousness will identify with a bodily function if the attention can be fixed upon it long enough and one can, for example, become one with one's own breathing.

Here, then, is the scientific explanation of the mystical practices of all ages in which the so-called separate entities of mind and body become directly unified in consciousness: voluntary-involuntary sensory channel overlap causes mental and physical awareness to merge in a single identity that is not perceived as either mind or body *because it is both simultaneously.*

We end this chapter with some meditation exercises and themes given in our training courses that may be useful in deepening and expanding your meditative state.

MEDITATION ON CANDLELIGHT

Visualize a candle burning; a tall, gleaming wax candle. See the blue inner and the golden outer flame; the thin plume of black smoke; the little pool of molten wax around the base of the flame. Now smell the burning wax, notice the flickering shadows; but above all, be aware of the brightness of the light. . . .

Imagine, now, the light being brought into your heart— just the cool, clear brilliance of the light. Imagine that light becoming brighter and brighter, shining up through you and illuminating your body. Now imagine it shining down through you, becoming still brighter; illuminating your whole body. Your whole body is alight and aglow, like a luminous figurine in purest crystal. . . .

Imagine another person filling with light . . . and another . . . and another, until the whole class has been
transformed to glowing golden crystal figures filling the
room with radiant splendor. See the walls, the floor, the
ceiling and every object in the room aglow. . . .

Now the room is filled to overflowing with a flood of
light, and the light is overflowing through the doors and
windows and out into the streets. . . . See the light running through the streets, filling people, vehicles and buildings with its joyous, golden brilliance. . . .

Now the whole earth is bathed in light. . . .

And the light fills the solar system and spreads into
outer space. . . .

And now the light fills the entire universe. . . .

THE SELF MEDITATION

I want you to picture yourself in a quiet place, seated at
the center of a bubble which represents your conscious
mind and also your *personal space,* that is, the free room
before you come in contact with any other person's personal space. See a delicate, rainbow-colored bubble just
enclosing you at head and heels, and imagine that this
space contains your consciousness—everything, internal
and external, of which you are at this very moment aware.
Now picture a larger bubble, perhaps the size of a
double-decker bus, to represent (to the same scale) your
preconscious mind, that is to say, everything which is not
present in consciousness but which can readily be
brought there by an effort of will (what you were doing
last night, where you spent your last birthday, whether
your right foot is warmer than your left, your own phone
number or that of a friend). Finally, picture a vastly greater
bubble the size of a cathedral, and concentric with the

other two. This represents the vastness of your unconscious mind (containing, among other things, all the forgotten memories of everywhere you have been, everyone you have met; all the books you have read, plays, films and TV shows you have seen; conversations you have heard; unpleasant experiences you would rather not remember). Notice that, in this configuration, everything comes to you through the intermediate stages of your unconscious and preconscious minds, and meditate that this is so. When you learn something in the usual *mediate* and *indirect* way, through your special senses and your reason, the perception is initially unconscious, because you are unaware of the operation of your sense organs and are only aware of the electrical changes which they induce in the appropriate regions of your brain. If you acquire *mystical* knowledge, that is to say, knowledge acquired *immediately* and *directly* (becoming the object of thought, as mystics would say), then that knowledge still arises through the unconscious mind. Meditate upon these three bubbles for a few minutes, and then meditate in this form: "I (that is, my real *I*) am not my physical body, but that which uses it, including its senses. I am not my emotions, but that which controls them. I am not my thought processes, but that which initiates and directs them. But I *AM*. What am I?"

GOLDEN WATERFALL MEDITATION

This is one of a number of traditional meditations which almost certainly originated in China and use images of *Ch'i* or vital energy as a means for cleansing, healing and revitalizing body and mind.

Visualize yourself seated upon a beautiful carpet of the kind which, in fairy stories and the Arabian Nights tales, are used for magical transportation. The carpet carries you high into a cloudless blue sky until, at an immense height, a vast waterfall comes into view, a waterfall of warm, golden light. Even at a distance, you can feel the power radiating from this waterfall. There is a limitless energy about it, matched only by its beauty. Slowly you approach the cascade itself and begin to feel the pleasant, warm tingle as drops of light pour over your head. The carpet carries you higher into the waterfall, and you stand up so that you are more fully exposed to the invigorating spray. The beautiful golden light pours down over the top of your head, passing through the skull at the back of the eyebrows, so that you light up with a gentle, golden inner glow. There is a faint sound as of cascading water. The warm golden light moves on to the nose, down to the lips and chin. It flows over the neck to the shoulders and chest, revitalizing and strengthening every part of your body that it touches. From the chest to the abdomen, and then the tanden, two inches below the navel. Here, let it rest for a few seconds, feeling the tingling, glowing warmth at this vital center. No thinking, no analyzing. Just silent awareness of the pool of *Ch'i* energy two inches below the navel.

Now we start the Golden Waterfall Meditation proper. Follow the sequence very carefully. Take the pool of golden *Ch'i* from the tanden* between the legs and start the flow of energy up the back. As the light moves upward along the spine, slowly inhale, bringing the breath to the top of the head along with the golden light. In order to make the process still easier, gradually raise the eyes (behind the closed eyelids), using the movement of the eyes and the breath like levers or ropes to draw the light up the back. When the golden light reaches the top of the head, we hold the breath with the eyes still tilted upward, letting the light bathe the whole of the skull. There is also

* See Glossary.

the patter of fresh drops of light coming from the golden waterfall. As the light begins to come slowly down the front again, gradually breathe out and lower the eyes. Finally, the breath is fully exhaled and the eyes looking downward as the *Ch'i* reaches the tanden, two inches below the navel. Here, with the breath out and the eyes cast down, we hold the tingling, glowing warmth. It is important in this meditation to keep the eyes closed and the spine properly erect. Move the pool of light *slowly*, with each cell of the body feeling the tingling, revitalizing energy as it passes.

Each movement of the pool of *Ch'i* from the tanden around the body and back to the tanden again is termed an *orbit*. The exercise should be performed in multiples of three orbits. Eighteen orbits is a good number to begin with; it will be quite enough if you are really concentrating on the details.

BEINGNESS MEDITATION

This meditation is an exercise in mystical experience, an exercise in imagination. Taken together with similar meditations which you will have in future sessions, it will become an exercise in self-knowledge.

I want you to see yourself as a bird.
What kind of bird are you?
Can you clearly see your colors, feathers, size, shape?
Are you domesticated or wild?
Do you follow the seasons, fly south in winter, or stay near
  human habitation?
How high do you fly, how fast?
What do you eat?
Do you have a mate?

What kind of a song or whistle do you have?
Are you afraid, timid? What makes you afraid, happy?

Do not try to rationalize too much, just feel all these things by trying your best to *be* a bird for the next few minutes. . . .

Now be a

tree
animal
fish
vintage car—type, color, make, year, condition, power
ship or boat—punt, canoe, rowboat, liner, warship
book in a library—paperback, hardback, fiction
famous historical figure
famous fictional character
the person in your life you would most like to be if not
    yourself.

These exercises were to be written up, one each week, for the first nine weeks. During the ninth week, the sequence is to be written up, with the students' own comments on what it reveals about themselves.

Chapter 4

The Fifth State
and the Mind Mirror

The more meditation is practiced, the easier it becomes to produce and to maintain alpha rhythm, and the longer continuous alpha rhythm is maintained, the more often the individual experiences states of higher awareness.

In EEG training for higher states of consciousness or awareness, the student, while endeavoring to maintain this alpha continuity, applies himself more and more to intellectual and emotional activity so as to infuse the calm, detached awareness of the alpha state into normal brain activity.

In this way, what Dr. Keith Wallace called the fourth state of consciousness leads on to become a fifth state of consciousness, or what we call lucid awareness, which is, on the psychophysiological level, a function of the waking state and the fourth state, but identical to neither.

The prototype experience of this lucid awareness (or awakened mind), is fourth-state awareness, but it is *coexistent with thought processes*. In other words, subjects walk about in

Isabel Cade and Swami Prakashanand on Mind Mirror, monitored and observed by Maxwell Cade and Geoffrey Blundell (standing).

Class in progress. Maxwell Cade facing.

what appears to be their normal consciousness, yet show the brain rhythms of other states.

We first identified this expanded realm of consciousness when our students carried over their alpha and theta states after training sessions, with their eyes open, for varying lengths of time, and when given further exercises, they often could extend these lengths of time quite considerably, despite distraction and the return to normal conversation and movement.

A subsequent period of two years further research and the training of about three hundred subjects with an average of three and a half hours training for each subject, during which the persistence, amplitude and frequency of their brain rhythms were checked over the spectrum from one Hertz to twenty Hertz, led to several new findings. It seemed that most researchers in this area had failed to note the simultaneous presence of other relevant frequencies in the fifth state— namely theta, beta or even delta waves.

Our work revealed the following significant factors:

1. All subjects, without exception, and usually at the first EEG training session, show a postmeditational phase in which continuous or almost continuous alpha persists for ten minutes or more with eyes open, provided the gaze is unfocused.

2. What at first sight appear to be two different kinds of alpha state turn out to be entirely different states. One of these is pure alpha, unaccompanied by more than a few percent of other frequencies. The characteristics of this state are as described by Dr. Kamiya and others— mindless, relaxed, neither thinking nor imaging. The other state shows high-amplitude alpha accompanied by two side bands of about 30 to 60 percent of the alpha amplitude, continuous and of steady frequency— one at usually 16 to 18 Hertz in the beta spectrum, the other usually at 4 to 6 Hertz in the theta spectrum.

   This special kind of alpha state is almost invariably bilaterally symmetrical, that is, showing the same amplitude and frequencies in both brain hemispheres. Subjects in this state can open their eyes, hold conversations with others and even walk around the laboratory carrying their EEGs while maintaining the state. They are able to solve simple mathematical problems in their heads, experience self-induced emotional states, read and understand literature—all without disturbance of the state.

   Usually, testing the state will result in its cessation after ten minutes or so, but it can invariably be restored by the subject adopting a passive attitude for a few minutes.

3. What we term lucid awareness (similar to Daniel Goleman's fifth-state consciousness) appears to exist over a

rather limited range of neurological arousal. It is difficult to produce hyperarousal in some subjects, but if this is successful, they pass into an ordinary beta state. Again, if left listening to music or contemplating some meditational theme, they do not remain in the bilaterally symmetrical EEG state but pass into a more asymmetrical state of theta or even delta-wave accompaniment. The skin resistance will then indicate a marked decrease in arousal level.

From this point, it was not illogical to propose the equation of this instrumented spectrum of states with those mystical states previously ascribed only to practitioners of esoteric religions and spiritual philosophies as when, for example, students relate a sense of illumination, bliss, union and, occasionally, indescribably beautiful visions. In fact, it was like listening to people who had never heard of biofeedback, people who spoke in extravagant terms long held suspect by psychoanalysts and psychiatrists, the medical profession, and certainly by scientists, who believed them to be distortions of the mind, defense or escape mechanisms of neurosis, schizoid manifestations of the brain, regressions into infantile or prenatal fantasies, and many other categories of aberration.

We jumped to no conclusions but went on experimenting. We continued to find confirmation of the lucid state and to help our subjects prolong it, keeping records of both machine monitoring and their spoken correlates of feeling and experience, not only in our sessions, but in the protracted effect in their daily lives (some of these descriptions are given at the end of this chapter).

Here are some of the training exercises we devised to develop this state in conjunction with the instruments (they can also be carried out without the machines, as extensions of the meditative state, by remembering the feeling of what one knows has been a successful meditation, and simply attempting to achieve extensions of the state):

1. Externalizing
    a. Open eyes, look slowly around room without focusing on anything.
    b. Focus eyes sharply on various objects.
    c. Make eye contact with other people.
    d. Mentally solve the following problems:
       (1.) $(7 \times 7) - (5 \times 5)$;
       (2.) $(11 \times 11) + (12 \times 12)$;
       (3.) ¾ of 160;
       (4.) $\dfrac{\frac{1}{2} (220 \times \frac{1}{2} (160/80))}{\frac{1}{4}}$

2. Sentic Cycles (based on the work of Manfred Clynes, in which the subjects successively experience self-induced sensations of: emotionlessness, anger, hate, grief, love, joy and reverence): For two minutes each, feel the following seven emotions. The sequence of seven states is called a cycle. If time permits, repeat the cycle twice.
    a. no emotion, just calmness
    b. anger
    c. hate
    d. grief
    e. love
    f. joy
    g. reverence

3. Stress Transcending—Pick up your EEG machine and walk about the room talking to people. Pause and rest with eyes shut if you lose the tone. Next, leave the room, walk downstairs and then return.

As a further extension of these exercises, we suggest some exercises that can be an effective means of fully awakening every sleeping sense, thereby enhancing and assisting lucid awareness and the achievement of higher states of consciousness. These are the exercises devised by the famous philosopher P. D. Ouspensky, a pupil of Gurdjieff. "Man," said Ouspensky, "is asleep. In sleep he is born, in sleep he lives and in sleep he dies. Life for him is only a dream, a dream from which he never wakes." Ouspensky was not speaking metaphorically; he meant that we are all living in a world inhabited by sleepwalkers who move about in a twilight of consciousness but believe themselves to be awake.

Ouspensky suggested a simple experiment to show whether we are really aware of ourselves. He recommended that we sit in a quiet place and look at the hands of a watch and see how long we can maintain the attitude of "I am sitting here, looking at the hands of a watch, and trying to remember myself."

It turns out to be extraordinarily difficult to do this for even one minute—to concentrate *only* on the idea of watching oneself watch the hands of a watch.

Another of Ouspensky's exercises is more obviously difficult but also more obviously valuable as being likely to help wake one up and expand one's consciousness. He recommends walking down a street and really using our eyes—not merely looking at the cracks in the pavement, but *seeing* the people, the traffic, the treetops, the chimney pots, the clouds, the birds. And also not seeing things as black and white or vague shades of gray, but in all the exciting colors they really show. Moreover, we should *really* look at things, as a child might on seeing them for the first time; not labeling them with sophisticated names and reasoning them away, but seeing them vividly, solidly, just as they *are*.

And then, when we are really as fully aware as we can be

of all the world of vision about us, he tells us to concentrate upon what we can *hear*—not just the passing traffic and the voices of people, but the songs of the birds, the hum of a distant airplane, the smack of our shoes on the pavement and the voice of the wind in the trees. (Again, we must not label these sounds, thereby sweeping them under the carpet of forgetfulness; but hear them freshly, just as they really *are*.)

Now, while being careful not to lose any of the sensory stimuli already flowing in from sight and sound, we bring in the world of odor and notice the smell of the earth after rain, the fragrance of flowers, perhaps the fumes from diesel engines and the whiff from the flueworks as well. (Again, we must not be obsessed with the sources of these scents; we must still the squirming of that mental worm of ratiocination and be content to accept them just as they *are*.)

Now we bring in the skin senses—where do we *feel* warm or cold? Notice the brush of your clothes against your skin, the impact of your shoes on the soles of your feet, the wind on your cheeks and the feeling of tension and movement in your muscles and joints. You can bring in taste and smell, too, if you wish, and suck a lemon drop or peppermint.

Now, for four or five minutes, attempt to pay equal attention to all these varied sensory inputs. When you have achieved what seems to be the best you can manage, maintain that degree of attention and at the some time count your steps along the road *and* recite some piece of poetry, say Kipling's "If" or the *Rubáiyát of Omar Khayyám*. No, it is not impossible to do all this, merely extremely difficult.

If you go through Ouspensky's exercise conscientiously, you will experience what amounts to a new altered state of consciousness—the state of generalized hyperesthesia, or mind expansion without drugs—and however successful or unsuccessful you were in focusing all the stimuli, provided that you made a really honest effort, you will realize why

Ouspensky said, "Man is asleep; for compared to what we are capable of, our normal waking state is more like sleep-walking."

Finally, we give the following meditation sequence, which should be preceded by the Meares relaxation sequence (see pp. 87–88) and the Zazen breathing method (see pages 95–96).

There is no such thing as time. It does not exist. There is only now. Only this present moment. Pay attention to your own internal sensations, to your environment, and to the presence of other people about you.

Now concentrate upon the sense of fellowship. Upon a feeling of being here-and-now with each other. Open your eyes and look at the other members of the group. Try to keep up a flowing eye contact and to develop the feeling of togetherness, while being aware that there is no time. No time within you, no time outside you. All of you just together in a timeless present moment.

This moment together *is* . . . This moment is eternal. . . . There never was a time when this moment was not going to be . . . There will never be a time when this moment has not existed . . . This unique part of eternity just is.

Now look at each other and at the furniture and all the objects in the room and try to see them as four-dimensional, as not only having height and length and width, but as having extension in time, too. See each one of us as long time-snakes, extending out of the room, out of the house, down the street and right back to home . . .

Now look at the walls, the door, the window. How far do they extend back in time? Fifty years? A hundred years? Picture their beginnings in workshops and builders' yards. Their erection here. Picture their fate when this building is eventually demolished.

Step out of ordinary time altogether. See everything and

everyone as world-lines stretching backward and forward in time. Then back to this unique here-and-now. There is only now. This moment *is*.

The relevance of such exercises to the attainment of higher states of awareness becomes clear when one remembers that the aim is not to become more wide awake nor more relaxed and dreamy, but to expand as far as possible the range of states over which one has full conscious control.

We have had many letters from pupils who learned the production of fifth-state consciousness in the classes and subsequently found how to use it in stressful situations in daily life. Busy housewives, an architect, a doctor, company executives and others with duty-filled lives told how they could center themselves, see the situation clearly and unemotionally and then cope with situational complexities and sheer masses of work that would have seemed impossible before they learned what the Flemish contemplative, John Ruysbrock, learned: "Then only is our life a whole, when work and contemplation dwell in us side by side, and we are perfectly in both of them at once."

TWO

Biofeedback and the Higher States

Chapter 5

The Hierarchy
of States

Once the fifth state, the awakened mind, has been reached, the instruments play a less well defined role. Here, one advances into sixth, seventh and eighth states of awareness, which are given a wide variety of names by modern psychologists and interpreters of higher consciousness who are in essence attempting alternative terminology for what is actually mysticism.

William James wrote that the two outstanding characteristics of the higher states of consciousness are "optimism" and "monism":

> We pass into mystical states from out of ordinary consciousness as from a less into a more, as from smallness into a vastness, and at the same time from unrest to rest. We feel them as reconciling, unifying states. They appeal to the yes-function more than to the no-function in us. In them the unlimited absorbs the limited and peacefully closes the account.

There are two other characteristics he might have added: first, the absolute conviction of truth which these states convey; impossible though the individual may find it to express in words what he has learned, he has no doubt whatsoever of its truth. Our ordinary knowledge is obtained through the functions of the special senses and the reason, but mystical knowledge is *direct* and *immediate* knowledge, as opposed to *indirect* and *mediate* knowledge, *inituitive* knowledge rather than *intellectual* knowledge.

Another major characteristic of the higher states of consciousness is the complete change which takes place in our sense of time, both in the timeless interval of the experience itself and in an altered attitude to time henceforward.

One of the illusions of many who long to press forward into these states is that they can somehow be "acquired," that there is some scientific process or psychological route they can simply follow and find themselves lifted forever out of ordinary states of consciousness, or what in the Bhagavad Gita is referred to as "the village of the senses." Nor are the higher states "entered" as one might walk into a room; they are the result of a gradual transformation of one's being, like the change of a caterpillar into a beautiful butterfly.

Basically, what is being transformed is one's level of awareness, not only of external reality but also of oneself. It is, perhaps, like gradually awakening from sleep and becoming more and more vividly aware of everyday reality—only now it is everyday reality (the Sufis' "waking sleep") from which we are awakening! The enlightened have spoken of this for thousands of years: the ancient Egyptians said, "The light is within thee, let the light shine"; the Buddhists say, "Look within; thou art Buddha"; Christ said, "I am the Way, the Truth, the Life."

And this gradual transformation takes continuous, diligent effort; it is not for the dilettante; one gets out of all the initial

Electrical Brain Rhythms of
Different Levels of Consciousness

Level		Mind Mirror patterns
8	Cosmic Consciousness Unity	?
7	Being Cognition—Maslow Psychedelia—Gowan Illumination—Bucke Self-remembering—Gurdjieff God Consciousness—Maharishi's sixth level	?
6	Creativity	
5a	Nirbikalpa Samadhi—Traditional Fifth State—Goleman Illumination—Fromm Cosmic Consciousness—Maharishi The Awakened Mind—Cade	β α θ
5b	Sabikalpa Samadhi—Traditional Lucid Awareness—Cade	
4	Fourth State—Wallace Meditation—Traditional Transcedental Consciousness—Maharishi	α θ
3	Waking Waking Sleep—Gurdjieff	β
2	Hypnagogic State	α
1	Dreaming Sleep	θ
0	Deep Sleep	δ

groundwork of transformation into the higher states of awareness just as much as one puts into it, and for many the effort
is hard and prolonged. Nothing can hurry it, nothing can
force it forward artificially, without the risk of undoing all the
genuine progress.

"Take a gear shift car out on the road," says J. C. Gowan
in *Development of the Psychedelic Individual* (1974),

> and while going at a slow speed in first gear, try to slip the
> gear into third or overdrive without going through second:
> the car will sputter and likely stall; this is akin to develop-
> mental forcing. Take the same car, "rev" it up to top speed
> in overdrive, then try to engage the car in the lowest gear.
> You will hear lots of noise and commotion, and maybe
> strip your gears; this is akin to developmental abuse. In
> both cases we are trying to do something unnatural, some-
> thing against the grain, something which will only result
> in injury to the car and poor performance.

Gowan also points out that developmental forcing, the effort to attain levels of consciousness for which the individual is
not prepared, is analogous to developmental abuse, the attempt to use the characteristic powers or fruits of a given
stage for display purposes when the individual is actually
engaged in tasks of a lower stage. For instance, his objections
to the use of psychedelic drugs as a means of achieving
higher states are:

1. Illegal or adulterated drugs of questionable purity may
   have damaging effects.

2. Bad trips or dissociated behavior may lead to physical
   harm or mental damage.

3. Future developmental progress may be impaired.

4. The "lotus-eaters" syndrome may take effect, in which the experience may prove so pleasurable that it distracts the individual from efforts toward valid growth.

Here, then, we will present some descriptions of the sixth, seventh and eighth levels of awareness, states that, despite evidence from the Mind Mirror, remain fundamentally ineffable territory.

But first, as a preliminary insight, let us consider the main difference between East and West in their accepted ways of gaining knowledge itself. The Eastern mystic seeks, through meditation, to empty his mind so that higher knowledge may be revealed to him. The Western belief is that knowledge comes only through observation and reasoning based upon observation. The mystic believes that knowledge can come directly to the mind, through intuition and revelation from within. These are very real and quite fundamental differences. We, as scientifically oriented Westerners, must accept the possibility that our familiar ways of knowing, while very plausible and logical, may not be the only ways, and perhaps not even the best.

Among Western scientists, there are widely divergent conceptions of the nature of *mind:* for the behaviorist and many psychoanalysts, mind is a repository of learned responses and memories; for the humanistic psychologist, mind is a computer, a simulator; and for some experimental psychologists, who propose "mentalistic behaviorism," mind is idea, which means that an idea implanted in the mind, no matter how that implantation is achieved, works continuously to manifest itself in external reality.

But in mysticism, ideas must cease, since only then, with the stilling of "the squirming of the worm in the brain," can one become filled from a higher source and attain full consciousness.

The characteristics of mystical states (what we term higher states of awareness) have been eloquently set out by F. C. Happold in *Mysticism* (1963) as follows:

1. First of all, a mystical state has the quality of ineffability, that is to say, it defies expression in terms which are fully intelligible to one who has not known some analogous experience.

2. Nevertheless, while mystical states are akin to states of feeling, they are also states of knowledge. They have a noetic quality. They result in insight into depths of truth unplumbed by the discursive intellect, insights which carry with them a tremendous sense of authority.

3. Mystical states can seldom be sustained for long; they rarely last for any length of time. They have thus the quality of transiency. There is invariably a speedy return to normality. The following of a particular way of life can, however, increase their frequency. At that stage of the Mystic Way known as the Illuminative Life, they can be very frequent and, it would seem, even controllable.

4. It is possible to prepare onself for the reception of spontaneous mystical experience. Indeed, in the writings of the mystics, much space is given to instructions on the following of the so-called Way of Purgation. Nevertheless, when they occur, mystical states invariably carry with them a feeling of something given. They have a quality of passivity. The mystic feels as if his own will were in abeyance, as if he were grasped and held by a power not his own.

5. A common characteristic of many mystical states is the presence of a consciousness of the oneness of everything. All creaturely existence is experienced as a unity,

as All in One and One in All. In theistic mysticism, God is felt to be in everything and everything in God.

6. A further characteristic of mystical experience is the sense of timelessness.

7. Bound up with the sense of oneness and the sense of timelessness, another characteristic of mystical experience is the conviction that the familiar phenomenal ego is not the real I. This conviction finds expression in one form in the Atman of hinduism in which the self, the ego of which we are normally conscious, is not the true self. It is conscious only by fits and starts; it is bound up with bodily organizations and mental happenings which are subject to change and decay; it is, therefore, only an ephemeral, phenomenal self.

In contrast to these definitions of mystical states are those of Andrew Weil, in his book *The Natural Mind* (1972), who uses the words "straight" and "stoned" as synonyms for the kind of thinking done by our everyday intellect compared with that available in the consciousness of "non-ordinary" reality, and lists the characteristics of ordinary attitudes as follows:

1. a tendency to know things through the intellect rather than through some other faculty of the mind

2. a tendency to be attached to the senses and, through them, to external reality

3. a tendency to pay attention to outer forms rather than to inner contents, and thus to lapse into materialism

4. a tendency to perceive differences rather than similarities between phenomena

5. a tendency to negative thinking, pessimism and despair

Andrew Weil illustrates the tendencies of the ordinary consciousness toward short-sighted materialism by the following examples:

1. excessive use of insecticides, leading to the widespread destruction of other life

2. excessive use of antibiotics, leading to the widespread development of resistant pathogens

3. allopathic medicine (treating symptoms by countermeasures, thus often leaving the causes untouched)

4. use of the allopathic model in psychiatry, and particularly the use of crude and often destructive measures, such as insulin shock, electroconvulsive treatment and leucotomy

5. political action as a crude means of producing change, and heavy-handed attempts to produce virtue by means of legislation

These comments lend themselves to argument, of course, but there is sufficient truth in them to provide contrast between nonordinary and ordinary states of awareness before passing on, finally, to enumeration of the ascending hierarchy.

To recapitulate the order we have dealt with: sleeping, (including the hypnagogic and hypnopomic states); waking, the relaxation response and meditation; the fourth state of consciousness; and the fifth state, a higher waking state in which continuous self-awareness is maintained in addition to awareness of the external environment, which we call lucid awareness or the Awakened Mind.

For the Sixth, Seventh and Eighth states, there are as many terms as there are philosophers and writers on the subject, and in order to arrive at those which are inclusive yet illustrative enough to be informative, we have chosen to call them, respectively, creativity and psychedelia, which means mind-manifesting, and cosmic consciousness.

We see the sixth state, creativity, as the prime area of higher creative development in that it opens up and gives access to a working relationship with what Carl Jung called the collective unconscious or group mind, wherein is stored all the unformed material of all human consciousness, the particularized manifestations of which we call individual consciousness.

On the Mind Mirror, the colored light pattern is seen as a slightly eliptical circle (extending from low theta to moderately high beta with its peak in the alpha region). For us, it has appeared infrequently so far, and usually with subjects who frequently experience state five, those who meditate as a way of life and those who spend a great deal of their time in some highly creative pursuit. Undoubtedly it exists in many more people than we know of, but until there are enough machines to make wide-scale measurements, we can only hypothesize about this.

Those who do attain this pattern often have an innate sense of the ineffable aspects of life, with accompanying emotions of being part of them, whether of a directly spiritual nature or simply in some nameless response; and though they may feel unified with something far vaster than themselves, they may not consider themselves mystics.

Or, on the other hand, they might be on some definite spiritual path, Western or Eastern, and may feel strongly unified with their particular concept of the ultimate essence of life. They might then be in an inner state of exaltation, peace and quiet ecstasy, and may feel in touch with limitless ideas and a limitless flow of creativity, and receive impressions of great beauty or value as well as new insights.

Once one has attained the creativity level, it will color all the lower levels. In Chapter 2, we described the experience of the hypnagogic level in becoming aware of imagery, but we could not make its value fully apparent until the achievement of creativity made full understanding possible.

Robert Louis Stevenson learned early in his life that he could "dream" complete stories and could go back to the same story on succeeding nights to give it different endings. He eventually trained himself to dream plots for his books (including the famous *Strange Case of Dr. Jekyll and Mr. Hyde*, which came to him in three sharp scenes, one of them splitting in two to give the central idea of a voluntary change becoming involuntary). And Jean Cocteau in *The Creative Process* (1952) tells how he dreamed that he was watching a play about King Arthur, later noting that it was an epoch and had characters in it about whom he had no documentary information. So challenging was the dream that it led him to write his *The Knights of the Round Table*.

Creativity may appear at the hypnagogic level in reverie, a state which has largely been neglected in scientific studies until very recently. Yet it is of unusual significance because of the imagery in which unconscious mental processes are revealed to the waking self as symbols, words or complex patterns. Hypnagogic imagery may be described as pictures or words which one does not consciously generate but which spring into the mind fully developed.

There are many well-known instances of these creative images which researchers in this area have described as more vivid and realistic than dreams, more like the flash of whole pictures illustrating matters seemingly unknown to the one experiencing the images, where important discoveries and creative solutions have been found.

The nineteenth-century German chemist Friedrich Kekule von Stradonitz told of a series of deep reveries which led to his theory of molecular constitution:

One fine summer evening I was returning by the last omnibus, "outside" as usual, through the deserted streets of the metropolis. . . . I fell into a reverie, and lo! the atoms were gamboling before my eyes. . . . I saw how, frequently, two smaller atoms united to form a pair, how a larger one embraced two smaller ones. . . . I saw how the larger ones formed a chain. . . . I spent part of the night putting on paper the sketches of these dream forms.

The last of this series of dreams led, in 1865, to Friedrich Kekule von Stradonitz's most famous discovery, which has been called the most brilliant piece of prediction in the whole range of organic chemistry.

I turned my chair to the fire and dozed. Again the atoms were gamboling before my eyes . . . long rows, sometimes more closely fitted together, all turning and twisting in snakelike motion. But look! What was that? One of the snakes had seized hold of its own tail, and the form whirled mockingly before my eyes. As if by a flash of lightning I awoke. . . .

In this manner, through the remarkable dream symbol of the snake biting its own tail, Friedrich Kekule von Stradonitz reached the notion that some organic compounds exist in closed rings. It is really not surprising that he urged contemporary scientists with these words: "Let us learn to dream, gentlemen"—though we would call his "dream" hypnagogic imagery or reverie.

In addition to these examples, there are hundreds of other anecdotes which show beyond doubt that, in some way which is as yet imperfectly understood, reverie, hypnagogic imagery and the related hypnapompic imagery are associated with creativity.

As for the relation between alpha and theta brain rhythms

and creativity, Albert Einstein, unquestionably one of the greatest creative geniuses of recent centuries, appeared to live in a semipermanent alpha state. Electroencephalographic studies showed that, quite unlike most people, Einstein could maintain continuous high-amplitude alpha while solving complex mathematical problems in his head.

As Professor Charles Tart has pointed out in *Altered States of Consciousness* (1964):

> The problem in studying the hypnagogic state in oneself or others is that the material experienced is generally forgotten rapidly, especially as subsequent sleep intervenes between experience and reporting. A simple method to overcome this . . . is to lie flat on your back in bed, as in going to sleep, but keep your arm in a vertical position, balanced on the elbow, so that it stays up with a minimum of effort. You can slip fairly far into the hypnagogic state this way, getting material, but as you go further muscle tonus suddenly decreases, your arm falls, and you awaken immediately. Some practice with holding the material in memory right after such awakening will produce good recall for hypnagogic material.

One reason for this upheld-hand technique is to help maintain a certain degree of voluntary muscle tension. It appears that total relaxation is not conducive to the maintenance of a consciously manipulable mind-body state, and that some slight physical tension or discomfort needs to be maintained. The hand-balancing method takes continuous effort in maintaining consciousness during a monotonous situation, and it is this feature of the method that is effective. This method corresponds to the maintenance of muscular tension and monotonous activity by Zen and Yoga practitioners.

The hypnagogostat machine mentioned above makes it

easier to work in situations other than in bed, and is more positive in awakening the hypnagogic subject. As the subject passes over into the sleeping phase, the sudden decrease in muscle tone results in the spring-loaded contacts closing and the sharp-sounding buzzer going off. Awakening, but still in the relaxed state of 15 on the ESR meter but not lower than 10, the subject resumes and learns to hold the creative reverie state.

In this situation, hypnagogic reverie often presents to consciousness long-forgotten material consciousness, vividly displayed in arrangements which the conscious mind might not have thought of, even were all the material available in the form of written notes or sketches. The paradox is that one is most likely to get really creative solutions to problems in mental states where the usual thinking ability is virtually extinguished.

At the waking level, we use the relatively gentle method of a flickering light as an aid to creativity training. Research has confirmed that in most people, the flicker stimulation, either with eyes closed or open, produces extraordinary responses in the brain. This is because a light signal causes a coded message to be distributed to its every part, although messages reaching brain regions remote from the visual area produce no response. It should be said again that there is some danger for epileptics, particularly with flickers in the beta range of brain rhythms of between 16 to 25 flickers per second, but in the alpha and theta ranges of from 4 to 12 flickers per second, there is definitely a generally applicable stimulation of memory and creativity.

The peculiar feature of flicker stimulation is that anyone looking at the light soon begins to see more than just a flicker. There is a sensation of movement, pattern and changing color. The unexpected bonus is that all the fantastic designs, movements, colors and sensations of bodily involvement are in the mind of the perceiver *and supply a clue as to his creative potential.* Generally speaking, the variety and vividness of impression is greater with visual thinkers than with verbal thinkers, and it is proportional to the person's potential creativity.

Margiad Evans, a novelist who underwent the flickering-light experience, described her sensations in A *Ray of Darkness:*

> Lights like comets dangled before me, slow at first and then gaining a furious speed and change, whirling colour into colour, angle into angle. They were all pure, ultra-unearthly colours, mental colours, not deep visual ones. There was no glow in them, but only activity and revolution.

The problem of what causes the sensory illusions during flicker stimulation has perplexed scientists a great deal. The ever-changing patterns may be subjective evidence for some kind of mental scanning process; a person experiencing the illusions of movement and color change is, in effect, examining the sweep of his own brain, seeking anything that might have meaning or value.

Whatever the exact mechanism by which flickering lights stimulate large areas of the brain, properly used, such stimulation has a genuinely self-expanding effect, enhancing awareness, arousing creative drive, stimulating memory and powerfully reinforcing other out-of-this-world exercises, hypnagogic reverie and meditation. The use of strobe lighting followed by led meditations employing fantasy seems to be particularly effective as a means of releasing creative potential.

Lastly, in the training for creativity, we include techniques of "time-span awareness," or memory.

Many people say, "Memory? Why should I bother to develop my memory?" One excellent reason is that memory is our *integration in time*. It is of little use being a well-integrated person one day and a poorly integrated individual the next. It is memory that supplies the connecting link between the chronologically separate parts of the self.

The Yogis of old had a saying: "Plan your day at dawn, and your year at New Year's Eve." Now, while this was part of the general training in being "mindful and self-aware," it was also something more important. It was part of the training in time-span attentiveness, a matter to which the Yogis paid careful attention.

We vary greatly in our time-span awareness. Some people know nothing beyond the here and the now, the very center of the fleeting moment. Others live their lives always in the light of eternity. The Yogic aim is to train oneself gradually to recall more and more of one's past life until the instant is always clearly related to the facts of the past, and equally clearly related to the aims for the future.

But this does not mean one should be obsessed with forethought and planning. The Yogis would have approved of the Christian attitude expressed in the words: "Sufficient unto the day is the evil thereof. Therefore take no thought for tomorrow." The aim is, at an unconscious level, to see the present moment as the most brightly lit part of a continuum which can be seen to extend backward and forward. All memory training, to be of real value to the individual, should be linked to this concept of one's awareness of time-span.

The factors which relate to memory are usually considered to be repetition, relative recency and emotional content (attention). But there are less well known factors which are also of great importance, notably state of arousal (the optimum being different according to whether you are attending to a simple or a complex task) and the attitude of mind prior to remembering.

Because both creativity and remembering are strongly related to hypnagogic states, in our training we begin by asking students (or subjects) to carry out certain exercises in both imagery and memory, which are given at the end of the chapter.

In our class work, we also give training for the increase of creativity as a development of monitored meditation. The Maharishi Mahesh Yogi has said of creativity that it consists of "turning away from the surface of our being, where most of us are content to dwell, and learning to appreciate the deeper levels of mind. This ability, in turn, depends on the ability of the individual to permit his mind to become perfectly still. One cannot see into the depths of a lake unless the surface of the water is still and calm."

This definition helps one understand why meditation is said to enhance creativity. The creative person is distinguished from his noncreative contemporary by his capacity for experience at hypnagogic and deeper levels. This is often characterized by an illuminating intuitive "flash" during meditation.

The development of creativity through the regular practice of meditation is progressive, though it varies greatly in rapidity from one meditator to another. Access to deeper layers of the mind is at first attained only during the practice of meditation itself, but as one becomes more experienced, the ability to attain the more remote depths increases, and ultimately every meditation is a magic journey to the storehouse of visions and ideas.

Thus the use and control of dreams, the fostering and developing of intuition, of creative insights, the creative flow of imagery and inspiration gained in reverie or trance states that dissolve the barriers of the limited, individual mind all lead to an opening out of human potentiality.

At this point of development the sixth state moves into the seventh state, the one we call psychedelia, or what Dr. Abraham Maslow, in *Toward a Psychology of Being* (1968), has termed self-actualization, and for which, as yet, we have no measurement, no physiological correlate or pattern; it is, for the present, beyond the machines. But based on what we have discovered and studied of the ascendent levels, we find Dr. Maslow's definitions to a large measure compatible with the state of higher awareness as it is felt and demonstrated by those who have climbed the hierarchical ladder via the machines and our training. We therefore quote, in part, his observations.

After studying many ordinary people who were nevertheless highly creative, Dr. Maslow found that it was necessary to distinguish between special talent creativeness and what he termed self-actualizing creativeness, which showed itself widely in the ordinary affairs of everyday life and which looked like a tendency to do all things creatively. Frequently, he observed, it appeared that the essential aspect of self-actualizing creativeness was a special kind of perceptiveness, of creative insight that had nothing to do with productivity or training.

Creativity of this kind is normal to most children, but the problem is how to remain creative after the main biological development is completed at sexual maturity. Those adults who manage to stay creative do so by a simultaneous search for greater mental health and for environments which stimulate their creativity.

Thus, self-actualization is defined by Dr. Maslow as the act or process of manifesting the capabilities for which one had the potentiality. "We must make an immediate distinction," he says, "between the ordinary motives of people below the level of self-actualization—that is, people motivated by basic (human) needs—and the motivations of people who are sufficiently gratified in all their basic needs and therefore are no longer motivated by them primarily, but rather by 'higher' motivations. The self-actualizing person is one who is: (a) sufficiently free from illness, (b) sufficiently gratified in his basic needs, positively using his talents and capacities, (c) motivated by some values which he strives for and to which he is loyal."

Further to these characteristics, we list here a few of Dr. Maslow's twenty-eight "testable propositions":

1. All self-actualizing people are devoted to some task, call, vocation or beloved work ("outside themselves"). "Generally," says Maslow, "the devotion and dedication is so marked that one can fairly use the old words calling, vocation or mission to describe their passionate, selfless, and profound feeling for their 'work.' We could even use the words destiny or fate."

2. In the ideal instance, inner requiredness coincides with external requiredness; "I want to" coincides with "I must."

3. Self-actualizing people have a strong sense of their good fortune in this ideal situation, of luck, of gratuitous grace, of awe that this miracle should have happened, or wonder that they should have been chosen.

4. At this level, the division of work and play is transcended; wages, hobbies, holidays, and so on must be defined at a higher level. Dr. Maslow says,

    It is quite obvious that with such people the ordinary or conventional division between work and play is transcended totally . . . if a person loves his work and enjoys it more than any other activity in the whole world and is eager to get to it, and to get back to it after any interruption, then how can we speak about "labour" in the sense of something one is forced to do against one's wishes?

5. Such vocation-loving individuals tend to identify with their work and to make it into a defining-characteristic of the self. It becomes a part of the self. Says Dr. Maslow,

> If one asks a Self-actualizing person "Who are you?" he tends to answer in terms of his calling, e.g., "I am a lawyer," "I am a psychologist," etc. In Self-actualizing subjects their beloved calling tends to be perceived as a defining characteristic of the self. It becomes an inextricable aspect of one's being.

6. This introjection means that the self has enlarged to include aspects of the world and that therefore the distinction between self and not-self (outside, or other) has been transcended. Says Dr. Maslow:

> Certainly, simple selfishness is transcended here and has to be defined at higher levels. So may a person with a great talent to protect, protect it and himself as if he were a carrier of something which is simultaneously himself and not himself. He becomes his own guardian.

Carl Rogers, in *On Becoming a Person*, also bases his impression of "fully-functioning" or self-actualized personalities upon personal and clinical observations rather than upon scientific research, and he sees creativity as one of the important implications of functioning fully. He sees these personalities as moving in the direction of the following goals:

1. increased openness to life and experience, with a reduction in defensiveness

2. increased interest in the here-and-now aspects of living; living in the present moment

3. increased awareness of both the internal and the external aspects of each new experience, in fact, a great increase in all-around awareness

Finally, this list of measurable characteristics quoted from J. C. Gowan would be common to both Carl Rogers and Dr. Maslow:

1. openness to life and experience
2. creativeness
3. integration, wholeness, unity of the personality
4. firm identity, autonomy, inner-guidance
5. great awareness, both internal and external
6. spontaneity, expressiveness, aliveness
7. detachment, objectivity
8. ability to love
9. clear, efficient perception of reality; no illusions

It would seem, therefore, that the path of self-maximization is one which is broad enough for many different kinds of people. For one individual, it will mean a continuous cycle of occasional creative flashes followed by longer rests; for another, genuine peak experiences accompanied by increase in power, energy and creativity; for a third, it may mean an opening between the conscious and the unconscious mind which either becomes habitual under certain stimuli or is amenable to control from the conscious side. None of these is to be preferred above the others. All have their value, both for the individual and for mankind.

Now we come to our eighth state (although more generally

known as the seventh state, our fifth state having intervened in the hierarchy), known generally as cosmic consciousness. Probably the most widespread influence on the definitions of higher states of consciousness has been that of Maharishi Mahesh Yogi's Transcendental Meditation. He defines the hierarchy of states of consciousness as waking, sleeping and dreaming (as well as altered states of waking, sleeping and dreaming), with the physiological correlates similar to those we have dealt with: transcendental consciousness (the fourth state), also known as restful alertness; and cosmic consciousness. It is the development of this field of pure consciousness that is the goal of all meditators.

In 1872, while visiting England, Dr. Richard Bucke, a Canadian psychiatrist in charge of a large hospital near London, Ontario, had a classical "mystical illumination," or experience of cosmic consciousness. This account of it is modified from one quoted by William James in his *Varieties of Religious Experience:*

> I had spent the evening in a great city, with two friends, reading and discussing poetry and philosophy. We parted at midnight. I had a long drive in a hansom to my lodging. My mind, deeply under the influence of the ideas, images and emotions called up by the reading and talk, was calm and peaceful. I was in a state of quiet, almost passive enjoyment, not actually thinking, but letting ideas, images and emotions flow of themselves, as it were, through my mind. All at once, without warning of any kind, I found myself wrapped in a flame-coloured cloud. For an instant I thought of fire, a great conflagration somewhere close by in that great city; the next, I knew that the fire was within myself. Directly afterwards there came upon me a sense of exultation, of immense joyousness accompanied or immediately followed by an intellectual illumination impossible to describe.

Among other things, I did not merely come to believe, but I saw that the universe is not composed of dead matter but is, on the contrary, a living Presence; I became conscious in my self of eternal life, but a consciousness that I possessed eternal life then; I saw that all men are immortal; that the cosmic order is such that without any peradventure all things work together for good, the good of each and all; that the foundation principle of the world, of all the worlds, is what we call love, and that the happiness of each and all is in the long run absolutely certain.

The vision lasted a few seconds and was gone, but the memory of it and the sense of the reality of what it taught has remained during the quarter of a century which has since elapsed. I knew that what the vision showed was true. I had attained to a point of view from which I saw that it must be true. That view, that conviction, I may say that consciousness, has never, even in periods of the deepest depression, been lost.

In his book *Cosmic Consciousness*, Dr. Bucke lists the following as characteristic of "the supreme experience":

1. An awareness of intense light. The individual has a sense of being immersed in a dazzling flame or rose-coloured cloud or perhaps rather a sense that the mind itself is filled with such a cloud or haze. In the East it is called the "Brahmic Splendour." Walt Whitman (himself listed by Bucke as one of the Illuminated) speaks of it as "ineffable light—light rare, untellable, lighting the very light—beyond all signs, descriptions, languages." Dante (also listed by Bucke as an Illuminated One) states that the experience is capable of "transhumanizing a man into a god" and gives a moving description of it in these lines from *Il Paradiso* of the *Divine Comedy*:

The light I saw was like a blazing river
A streaming radiance between two banks

Enameled with wonders of the Spring
And from that streaming issued living sparks
That fell on every side as little flowers
And glowed like rubies in a field of gold.
Fixing my gaze upon the Eternal Light
I saw enclosed within its depths,
Bound up with love together in one volume,
The scattered leaves of all the universe:
Substance and accidents, and their relations
Together fused in such a way
That what I speak of is one single flame.
Of that Exalted Light saw I three circles
of three colours yet of one dimension
And by the second seemed the first reflected
As rainbow is by rainbow, and the third
Seemed fire that equally from both is breathed.

2. With the sensation of light the individual seems bathed in an emotion of joy, assurance, triumph, "salvation."

3. In addition to these sensory and emotional experiences there comes to the person an intellectual illumination quite impossible to describe. In an intuitive flash he has an awareness of the meaning and drift of the universe, an identification and merging with creation. He obtains a conception of the *whole* that dwarfs all speculation and imagination.

4. A sense of immortality.

5. With illumination the fear of death falls off like an old cloak—not, however, as a result of reasoning—it simply vanishes.

6. Loss of the sense of sin; the individual no longer sees that there is any sin from which to escape.

7. The instantaneousness of the illumination is one of its most striking features. It can be compared with a dazzling flash of lightning.

8. The character of the man who enters the new life is an important element in the case.

9. Subsequently there is a charismatic change in personality.

This extraordinarily rational account of a supernormal experience, while tallying closely with those of Western writers such as Aldous Huxley, Thomas Merton and many others who have attempted to describe similarly transporting and rapturous events in their lives, also matches every mystical description of this state, East or West and every age.

Saint Paul called it "the peace that passeth understanding." In Zen, the term for it is "Satori" or "Kensho"; in Yoga, "Samadhi" or "Moksha"; in Taoism, "the Absolute Tao"; and the Sufis speak of "Fana." G. I. Gurdjieff called it "objective consciousness"; the Quakers call it "the Inner Light"; Catholicism speaks of the "unio mystica." But whatever name it is given, there is no divergence in the descriptions of its affective power: it can be, and is, studied with total life-absorption by eminent scholars, as well as those untold millions of seekers who aspire to know it for themselves; yet this exalted realm of awareness, no matter how rare in actual achievement, forms a body of evidence as reliable phenomena of science.

Now, at last, we come to the subtle upward divisions of cosmic consciousness, beyond the so-far measurable. In his book about Transcendental Meditation, *The Seven States of Consciousness* (1973), Dr. Anthony Campbell describes them (as sixth and seventh states respectively in his hierarchy) in this way:

God consciousness is a logical development of cosmic consciousness. Cosmic consciousness is permanent awareness of the Absolute on the subjective level . . . the

Absolute does have features on account of which it could reasonably be called "God." First, it is consciousness itself, and in this sense is alive. Second, union with it is described as transcendental "bliss"—the "peace that passes all understanding." Third, it arouses feeling of the holy and the sacred. Fourth, it is the source of all values and all goodness. . . . Fifth, it differentiates itself into the phenomenal world by its own power, not as a temporal but as a timeless and eternal activity. . . .

Descriptions of Unity undoubtedly sound strange. This is because our language is adapted to frame either-or statements. We can say that things are many or that they are one, but what the mystic—the person in Unity—perceives is that they are *both* many *and* one. This cannot be expressed in words without contradiction.

Finally, what we see as a result of attaining all these higher states of awareness in successive steps, first by instrumented training and then by a process of self-remembering of those states, is that these even higher divisions that follow can be practically combined with the lesser ones. They do not have to be separated into opposing departments of happiness versus suffering, nonattachment versus involvement, but can be fused to make an integrated consciousness in which both the outer and the inner experience of life are more harmonious and successful.

Following are some examples of time-span Meditation, preceded by a relaxation technique.

1. First relax (the Ainslie Meares relaxation sequence, see p. 87, can help bring the subjects into the mind-body correlation of reverie). Now exercise both your imagery and capacity for fantasy with the meditation on the moon that follows.

2. Follow that with the meditation Journey Through Time (to appropriate music).

3. Return to the present; recall your own lifetime on the way. Maintain deep relaxation.

4. Sheehan and Lesh ratings.

THE MOON
(based upon a theme of Hari Prasad Shastri)

I am the Moon that travels the skies;
High above Earth, detached, serene,
I pour on the world my silvery light.
I see babes in their cradles in soft, happy sleep;
I see and pass on . . .
I see lovers parted by wars and strife;
Children torn from their parents' arms;
I see and pass on . . .
I see beautiful gardens with fountains and flowers;
Buddhist temples and Christian shrines;
Palm trees swaying and coral atolls;
I see and pass on . . .
I see teeming ghettos and desert wastes, tropical forest
    and Arctic snow; vast continents with soaring moun-
    tain ranges,
And sun-kissed islands lapped by gentle waves;
I see and pass on and on . . .
I see politicians intriguing and generals planning strategy;
Poets toiling at their rhymes, shepherds tending their
    flocks;
I see gardeners caring for rare blooms and sailors defying
    the seas;

I see starlings migrating and snails sleeping on mossy
  walls;

I see and yet pass on and on and on . . .

I am the Moon that travels the skies;

High above Earth, detached, serene,

I pour on the world my silvery light.

JOURNEY THROUGH TIME

Imagine yourself sitting comfortably and at ease on a river bank watching the clouds far up in the sky as they drift
past, forming and reforming their great, hazy shapes.
Gradually, you feel caught up in them, drifting along with
them, higher and higher, farther and farther; you seem to
be carried with them into a completely new dimension.

Your mind's eye now has the sense of a different focal
point. You relax into it, allowing yourself to feel this distant dimension pulling you strongly into itself, whirling
you through space at great speed, whirling, whirling, with
you in its center. You feel relief that the burden of voluntary control is lifted from you. You just relax, let yourself
go, deeper and deeper into its mysterious depth.

Now you become aware of the nature of this new dimension. It is a new time dimension, in which you can
travel backward or forward in terms of your ordinary time.
You become aware that you are traveling backward, backward, through the 1960s, '50s, '40s and '30s; through the
Roaring Twenties and World War I; past 1909, when
Blériot made the first cross-channel flight; and past 1903,
when Orville and Wilbur Wright made the first flight in a
heavier-than-air machine. Beyond the turn of the century;
for a flashing moment you are aware of the wonderful
year 1896, when Marconi first demonstrated wireless on

Salisbury Plain, the Nobel Prizes were established, and the very first British motor car amazed the public. Backward and backward, to 1891, when Conan Doyle published the first of the Sherlock Holmes stories; 1877, when Victoria was made Empress of India; 1876, when Alexander Graham Bell invented the telephone; 1840, when Victoria married Prince Albert, and 1834, when Peel, who initiated the Irish constabulary, was prime minister. Faster and faster: back to 1833, when the S.S. *Royal William* made the first full-steam crossing of the Atlantic; 1825, when Stevenson completed his famous railway engine, The Rocket. Past 1805, and the death of Admiral Nelson at the Battle of Trafalgar. Faster and faster still, backward and backward through time, back to the middle of the eighteenth century, to 1752, when Benjamin Franklin invented the lightning conductor; back to 1740, when Wesley composed "Hark the Herald Angels Sing," the Hell Fire Club flourished at Medenham Abbey, and George II was on the throne of England. Even faster, backward into the past, to 1685, the death of Charles II, and beginning to slow down at last as you come to 1609, when Galileo is credited with making the first telescope, which was really invented the year before, 1608, by Hans Lippershey. Slowing down now, 1605, the Gunpowder Plot and the capture of Guy Fawkes; 1603 and the death of Elizabeth. Still slowing down, you pass 1590 when Spencer produced perhaps his most famous poem, *The Faerie Queen*; 1570, when Elizabeth was excommunicated by Pope Pius V; past 1565, when Sir Walter Raleigh introduced tobacco into England; and 1564, when the very first horse-drawn carriage was introduced into England from Holland. Almost stopped now, you pass through seven more years and arrive at 1556, when Cranmer, Archbishop of Canterbury, was burned at the stake . . . through 1555 to 1554, with the execution of Lady Jane Grey and Lord Dudley; one more year, as you finally come to rest . . . in 1553.

You are in England in the year 1553. There are no airplanes, motor cars, railway engines—not even horse-drawn carriages. No electric light or gas. No television, radio or even a record player. The Duke of Northumberland has forced Lady Jane Grey, in line of succession to the throne, to marry his son, Lord Guildford Dudley. You are in the Banqueting Hall of the great palace at Hampton Court. The year is 1553, in the reign of Edward VI; 1553. . . . live the life of the time.

SHEEHAN'S MENTAL IMAGERY SCALE (1967)

	Rating
Perfectly clear and as vivid as the actual experience	1
Very clear and comparable in vividness to the actual experience	2
Moderately clear and vivid	3
Not clear or vivid but recognizable	4
Vague and dim	5
So vague and dim as to be hardly discernible or recognizable	6
No image present at all, only knowing that you are thinking of the object	7

NOTE: As applied to Vizualization Sequences, this scale has to be matched to (1) visual imagery, (2) touch, pain, heat and cold (skin senses), (3) taste and smell, (4) sound, (5) kinesthesia (sensation of bodily movement).
The score can vary, therefore, from $5 \times 1 = 5$ to $5 \times 7 = 35$, where the higher the score, the poorer the mental imagery.

Chapter 6

Biofeedback
and the Psi State

Psychic experiences may occur to an individual at any level of development, but unlike the hierarchy of states of awareness, they are not achieved in a developmental sequence, that is, they do not assist one up the rungs of the ladder. Their occurrence is simply a potential of the total human experience—a part of it that remains a challenge to ordinary reason and logic.

On the other hand, through awareness training and alterations of consciousness, one may become sensitive to the nonordinary reality in which they appear to occur, become more attuned, more receptive and more open to their occurrence, as has been shown in our class and laboratory work with simple experiments such as sending a subject out of the room and hiding a small object like a ring; then bringing him back in, connecting him to monitoring instruments and asking him to find it by means of his instrument-tone indication (which means that the instruments are making the subject aware of normally unconscious perceptions).

During a course we call Hypnopsychedelics, the term we coined to denote a system of training which embraces both voluntary control of internal states and experimental parapsychology, some simple experiments to determine the nature of "psi-conducive" states were carried out on students under various of the following conditions:

1. after student has just arrived in class and sat down
2. after ten minutes of autogenic relaxation
3. after ten to fifteen minutes of led meditation
4. after induction of hypnotic rapport
5. after induction of "group-mutual" hypnosis
6. after ten minutes of listening to gentle music
7. after empathy exercises
8. after various combinations of the above

The psi tasks which the subjects were required to undertake were as follows:

1. Zener-card* guessing
2. precognitive guessing of a picture or object not yet chosen
3. telepathic awareness of a picture, object or theme transmitted by an agent in another room
4. postcognitive guessing of a picture or object which was on display before the commencement of the class
5. raising or lowering hand temperature in accordance with instructor's telepathic command

---

* a pack of 25 cards marked with five different designs—a square, a star, waves, a circle and a cross.

6. using alpha-blocking response (as shown by the cessation of tone from audiofeedback EEG) to locate a concealed object

7. automatic drawing or automatic writing while conscious attention focused upon a poem read by class leader and agent(s) outside room concentrating upon impression to be transmitted while in an EEG-monitored alpha state

Zener-card guessing was the principal means used for investigation psi-conducive states of consciousness. The class leader called the cards as he looked at them, saying: "Card one . . . card two . . . card three . . ." and allowing about five seconds for the subjects to record their guesses (cross, square, circle, star or wavy lines).

Sometimes the correct description was called before the next guess, so as to provide immediate feedback, and this did appear to improve the guessing levels irrespective of the subjects' conscious states.

Over a period of two terms (twenty seminars), there were sixty series of card guessing, some using a single pack of twenty-five cards and sometimes using a double pack with ten cards removed at random. The mean results for all trials were as follows (chance level = 25 correct guesses):

1. normal waking state (just arrived in class)   24
2. after ten minutes of listening to music   25.7
3. after *either* five minutes of autogenic relaxation exercises or the empathy exercise   27
4. after ten minutes of led meditation   28.5
5. after hypnosis or group-mutual hypnosis   29
6. after five minutes of relaxation sequences, ten minutes of led meditation and the empathy

exercise (imagining enclosing bubbles as in
SELF MEDITATION on p. 98).   32

Other psi tasks did not lend themselves so readily to ad-
ministration, and there was little difference between the
methods of changing consciousness from normal. All the
methods showed an improvement as compared with the normal waking state.

What became immediately apparent was the strength of *individual* differences in psi ability at all tasks. The investigation therefore shifted to a study of the physiological correlates
of good performers as contrasted with poor performers. In
particular, a study was made of the relaxation response (using
the change in skin resistance as the index of relaxation) and
of the alpha, beta and theta brain rhythms, using an EEG
monitor.

It was immediately apparent that the good performers differed from the others in that they spontaneously relaxed
much more deeply (changes in palmar skin current of the
order of 65 to 85%, as compared with 40 to 60% in the poor
performers); and that they showed much more continuous
and stronger alpha brain wave activity (10 to 15 microvolts or
more, compared with 5 or less for the poor performers).

A policy was adopted of finding those consciousness-altering exercises which most facilitated the good performers'
entry into the psi-conducive state, and of encouraging the
poorer performers to spend more time in alpha-theta training,
relying on the well-established principle that the more these
states are experienced, the easier they are to produce at will.

Subjects were asked to use the EEG training equipment to
the full, switching themselves from alpha training to theta
training, and from left-brain hemisphere to right-brain hemisphere, until they could produce a high level of both alpha
and theta activity in both hemispheres. From time to time, a

trained operator would check progress and also monitor beta- and delta-wave activity, just for the sake of completeness of records.

During the progress of this work, a number of observations were made which suggested that whenever individuals showed what seemed to be extrasensory perception (ESP), they exhibited an unusual degree of voluntary control (e.g., simultaneously making one hand hotter and the other cooler) or made an exceptionally creative response, they frequently showed a fifth-state pattern.

The most remarkable effects observed with subjects in the active fifth state were in the form of paranormal communication. The experiment was tried of sending a subject in the fifth state (in the original tests, a subject producing high-amplitude continuous alpha waves) out of the room while an object was hidden somewhere in the classroom. The other subjects were asked to avoid looking at the hiding place but to keep it in mind. The "sensitive" had to find the hidden object solely by using his alpha-blocking response. When he reentered the room and walked around, his alpha production (as indicated by the note from the headphones or loud-speaker) would become irregular or sometimes cease when he was near the object.

In more than fifty of these tests, only four times did a subject fail to show the alpha-blocking response when near the concealed object. However, showing the response (and understanding that the object must be very close) was not the same as finding it. Several subjects consistently failed to look in the right place even when they knew that the place was within arm's reach. Three subjects (all producers of well-defined fifth-state rhythms) went almost straight to the hiding place and found the object every time.

Two subjects who had developed great ability to control their skin temperature at will, even to the extent of raising the temperature of one hand by two degrees Centigrade while simultaneously lowering the temperature of the other hand by a similar amount, took part in tests to see whether, while showing fifth-state brain rhythms, they could vary their skin temperature in accordance with a *telepathic* command. The seven orders (both hot; both cold; no change; left hot; right cold; right hot; left cold) were selected randomly and changes of command given telepathically at five-minute intervals. Both subjects were given immediate verbal feedback as to whether or not they had followed the order correctly.

One subject, Richard P., showed correct responses with both hands seven times out of ten; the other, Peter Y., showed correct responses with both hands six times out of ten. On another occasion, however, both were right only five times out of ten, although experimental conditions were unchanged.

Mystics in the state of cosmic consciousness have generally accepted experiences of events outside ordinary concepts of time and space as natural, as synonymous with their expanded consciousness of reality. They consider them unremarkable, useful, in fact, as a periphery benefit, but never as a means of gaining power or acclaim, and certainly never in attempts to prove truth or the existence of ultimate reality. This would be like those in the state of ordinary reality attempting to establish superiority and the fact of some invisible power because they could crack their knuckles or wiggle their ears.

For this reason, paranormal ability and psychic events can be seen as concomitant of the seventh stage of development, but occurring randomly in lower levels. Here, however, in altered states of perception such as are produced in most forms of meditation and trance, hypnosis, sensory deprivation, sleep loss, before and after sleep states, daydreaming, deep preoccupation—in fact, all these states where everyday consciousness is temporarily suspended or changed—the personal self may get out of the way and thus provide a climate for the occurrence of psychic phenomena.

These concepts are so alien to our ordinary state of consciousness (mainly because science has not yet been able to explain the principle of paranormal events to its own satisfaction, let alone that of the general public), that it may be quite difficult to accept them, even though it may be clear that some radically new approach is needed in order to explain the observed facts.

Although mediumistic trance is an altered state of consciousness that appears to be accompanied by the manifestation of paranormal abilities, very little has been published on the physiological changes which take place in mediums while they are in the trance state. When, therefore, we were invited to assist in some experiments organized by the Survival Research Trust in 1974–75, the opportunity was gladly accepted.

Just as with the experiments on yogis and Zen monks reported earlier, one found the early stages of trance to be accompanied by alpha waves which increased in amplitude and decreased in frequency. And this stage was followed by the appearance of theta waves and often by delta waves as well.

The decrease in frequency of the brain rhythms was accompanied by a steady and marked increase in skin resistance as long as the medium was in a state of passive trance, but this changed to a large *decrease* in skin resistance, corresponding to a large degree of hyperarousal, but without any change in the brain rhythms, as soon as the control began to communicate.

These findings were repeated with several well-known mediums, leaving no doubt that mediumistic trance is an "ecstatic" state, physiologically measurable: the brainwaves of the medium in trance are in a theta-delta range (sleeplike), while the body is highly aroused.

There remains much to be investigated in this vitally significant contrast of mind-body state, which makes us wonder what the early researchers in mediumship could have accomplished with biofeedback: perhaps the connotations of spuriousness that damaged excellent work would never have arisen.

Moreover, even if telepathy, telekinesis, clairvoyance and precognition all prove to be unreal, there are still wonderful potentials in the perfectly normal but usually undeveloped mind powers such as those shown by "memory men," calculating prodigies and the various people who, whether they call themselves yogis or not, can control pain as Mahatma Gandhi could, or walk on fire like Kuda Bux. These supposedly paranormal feats are nonetheless remarkable for having recently been equaled or approached by quite ordinary people using the modern technique of biofeedback.

Chapter 7

Training in the Higher Reaches of Meditation (Science of the Soul)

As our research with the Mind Mirror and the fifth state gathered more and more evidence of the significance of brain-hemisphere EEG symmetry, we expanded our meditation training to incorporate the study of meditation itself, that is, meditation without "seed," without any mystical or religious purpose, and to introduce more specific exercises for recognition of the quality of left- and right-brain hemisphere activity.

The course we devised for this purpose is intended for those people who have already completed the first two courses and are well-oriented in biofeedback self-control but want to go on practicing their skills and developing their understanding of what both they and the machines are doing.

Calling the course Methods of Meditation, we start each session with a descriptive talk on one or another of the traditions, for example, the Buddhist, Sufi, Zen or Yogic way (several of these talks on the various traditions can be found at the end of the chapter).

We explain neutrally and objectively the aims of each, the beliefs, the disciplines—not as instruction in the traditions themselves, for this would be outside our field and far better given in definitive individual study, but so as to relate the interior science of the traditions to their physical counterparts.

After this, with students connected to their machines, we give the students one of these traditional meditation methods to do experientially, using that method to induce the meditative state.

Following this, we talk again about the effect of this particular method on both hemispheres of the brain and on the nervous system, after which we demonstrate this with an experienced student on the Mind Mirror, explaining when a meditation is a transcendent one or a meditation exercise for the left or right hemisphere.

Our next step is to give meditative exercises to the class which will assist them to discriminate between left- and right-brain hemisphere functioning. For instance, since the left hemisphere is for categorizing, we might give them one of the meditations of Patanjali in which he asks you to sit quietly and listen to all the noises going on around you and just put a label on them: "that's the squeal of a tire, that's the bark of a dog, that is a voice in another room, that is wind in the trees outside, that is dishes being rattled, that is someone going upstairs," and so on.

For the right hemisphere, among the many exercises one might do to experience holistic perception is to imagine Nelson's column—"you are looking at it from one particular corner of Trafalgar Square"—and then, without using any words, imagine yourself walking around the square and notice the changing aspects of each side of the square in an inclusive way.

For using neither "left" nor "right" brain specifically but in fusion, we might use a meditation for being aware of everything that is going on around you, but not paying any actual attention to it at all. (Some of the meditations given earlier in the book may be used here; for other examples, see the end of this chapter.)

It is interesting to note that although meditation may be taught instrumentally for the purposes of deep relaxation, development of extreme self-awareness, gaining self-control and achieving a generally calmer, more creative and poised center, with its concomitants of improved health and energy, it may also induce what might be called soul consciousness. We feel we can tie this in with the beginning of brain symmetry, with Jung's "transcendent" function, for the common denominator of all traditions of meditation is their transcendence of the ordinary waking level, the field of relativity and the transience of life, to the "absolute." Here, then, is the physiological correlate of that junction where the mind travels from the relativity of everyday human life into all that is ultimate and changeless.

In describing his individual experience of training with us, one man in his late thirties, a sculptor and teacher of art, said:

After having overcome many long-standing problems with myself and my work through this broader spectrum of biofeedback training, I became very interested in meditation itself, the following of reveries and other aspects I was taught, and much more interested in climbing up the ladder of consciousness . . .

I've always had a sense of higher self, particularly when I'm involved with my work, when I feel the artist in me is of a different order than the ordinary person and takes over. Now I can identify it more tangibly with a higher, more knowledgeable self . . . I no longer revert to periods of doubt and cynical atheism, even if I get out of touch with the higher self for a while—I know the higher self is still there. So it's confirmed something: there is this intuitive self that operates on feelings, and that intuitive self in turn seems to be in touch with a universal spirit or collective unconscious . . .

In classes, when I'm on the Mind Mirror, I can more or less maintain fifth state as long as I keep my eyes closed, and sometimes with eyes open I will flip into sixth state. I've had strongly altered states with visions and a sense of spiritual communion. I find the whole classes in Methods of Meditation mystical, and I've had very brief peak experiences where everything I know is blotted out, all imagery . . . and others where I would find myself shot off into another dimension altogether as it were, with an after-effect of physical well-being and energy and general kindness towards humanity. . . .

Another student, a quantity surveyor in his fifties who had undergone a great deal of psychotherapy before coming to the classes, describes some of the feelings he experienced when he had advanced to the Mind Mirror:

It terrified me to begin with because it's an instant illustration of what your brain pattern is, so I deliberately relaxed my muscles, knowing by now that relaxation and anxiety are absolutely incompatible, and kept my eyes closed. It was easier to produce alpha that way and be indifferent to the fact that I was being monitored and watched. I don't think I ever attained a fifth state, but I became more deeply aware, and what made me aware was the philosophy, the Zen concept being used to evoke awareness, and it was the exercise and the practice of that that began gradually to make me even more aware and to want to further my reading on that aspect of meditation.

My philosophical outlook has greatly altered. The intrinsic worth of my job, compulsive striving to succeed in it, is to some extent dissolved . . . and nowadays I feel strongly that the quickest and most efficient way of getting rid of anxiety altogether is to involve physiological processes like relaxation and mental training in what are essentially Eastern disciplines. . . . In this very relaxed state in which the mind is still working on an intellectual level, other faculties are being brought in as well. The meaning isn't forced on one, but I was able to grasp quite intuitively the inner meaning of what was being taught, and not through a process of ratiocination.

More definitive experiences of soul consciousness are described here by a bookkeeper-typist in her late thirties:

From the first time I saw that needle responding to what I felt, the excitement started. The improvement in my life began almost immediately after I began training—the irritation, aggressiveness, anxiety—I am content now, I feel I can cope with anything that comes along now. If a saucepan falls on my head, well, that's okay by me . . . which is quite different from before!

I got to the fifth state too easily at first, then lost it, then gained it again as I began to understand more what was happening. I could then walk around in it with my eyes open and do arithmetic sums. But there's a lot of euphoria, a lot of joy with it, a feeling that one is at one with the universe. I hesitate to use the word divine, or spiritual, but there are higher links, somehow, coming straight through from something that one just knows is much purer and greater, and that you are a part of it . . . dancing the dance of life is the nearest way to describe it. One is terrifically aware of everything, one's own feelings as well as other people's, one is almost telepathic.

I had this particular experience after one of the lessons, having been filled with a great joy during the journey home. I recorded it in words.

There is a silver filament running right through the center of time. Mostly I am barging around on either side of it, but occasionally I cross this silver strand and marvel at its efficiency, strength and purpose. Its vibrations are so pure they have the sound of tiny bells; their sound is so beautiful I am amazed I can leave them, and, leaving them, not notice that I have left until, once again, I return. This strand is the Master of Masters, leading, inexorably, with no wastage, right through the center of the Universe. It links all and is linked to all; the microcosm and the macrocosm, horizontally, vertically, historically, futuristically—all in one perfect moment—*now*—held together *now* in this inner core of the spinal canal. I have a feeling that if I trained myself to stay here and follow its sound through the grass of my life, trace its silver line glinting, it might turn to gold.

Here is another experience I had after an exercise that posed the question, "How can I rid myself of negative feelings?" This answer came to me:

Negative feelings are the acids that eat away will and purpose. If the will/purpose aspect of one's being is to be awakened and in daily use, then negative feelings must be acknowledged and discarded. Will cannot operate without purpose. Purpose will not be apparent while inner sight is clouded by negative thoughts. Being is also apparently at the mercy of one's negative feelings; it involves both mind and heart action in unison, and that is why negative thinking has such an obvious and appallingly destructive effect on life. If one could remove negativity entirely from one's makeup, then add unclouded purpose—which automatically attracts to itself its other half, will—then what could one *not* achieve! In this vein, I wrote:

Be, My Child,
In Light and Love.
Be My Joy.

Be in Light
and shine my Joy

Be in Love
and sing My Joy.

Just *Be* in Light and Love, My Child
Praise Me for Joy.

These are not the descriptions of Eastern mystics but of ordinary people taking the courses and becoming deeply aware, deeply attuned to higher levels of consciousness.

In one study, jointly organized by ourselves and His Divinity Swami Prakashanand Saraswati, founder of the International Society of Divine Love, who was visiting our laboratory, we attempted to demonstrate the objective effects of the Divine Love Meditation upon the state of consciousness of various persons who had different degrees of experience with other forms of meditation or none at all. The swami had also asked for subjects' backgrounds to vary from sceptical businessmen to keen students of yoga. (Altogether we were able to work with him for seven weeks in early 1977.)

The Divine Love Meditation is a devotional meditation intended to increase the concentration of divine love in the heart and mind of the practitioner. The technical procedure is to monitor both the ESR and the EEG patterns continuously, using the Mind Mirror for the latter. Subjects were seated at laboratory benches, all of them with individual ESR meters and three at a time wired to Mind Mirrors (there were only three Mind Mirrors available at that time). A tape recording of Divine Love Meditation chanting was played, and the swami instructed students to listen with their hearts (that is, to respond emotionally rather than intellectually).

There were two twenty-minute sessions, so that those who had laboratory duties to perform could also have their turn.

Reports on Individuals

HILDA HART

Had been meditating for six months with concentration on the eyebrow chakra (see Sanskrit glossary). During the Divine Love chanting, she felt a softening in the heart and felt that she was listening in the heart with a very happy feeling

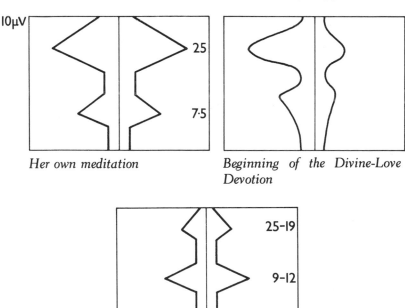

Her own meditation

Beginning of the Divine-Love Devotion

Divine-Love Devotion

which she had not found before. Her skin resistance rose from 500 kilohms per centimeter squared to 1.25 megohms per centimeter squared (60% relaxation response). Her previous EEG showed strong, symmetrical beta peaks (10 microvolts at 25 Hz) and weaker alpha peaks (5 microvolts at 7.5 Hz). During Divine Love Meditation, she showed reduced beta activity (5 microvolts) with alpha peaks at 9 to 12 Hz and theta peaks at 4.5 to 6 Hz. This represents a shift from shallow meditation to state-five consciousness.

MICHAEL ROBERTS

A professional, very reserved man who had never meditated before. He began with skin resistance of 480 kilohms per centimeter squared, which, during Divine Love Devotion, increased to 2.5 megohms per centimeter squared (80% relaxation response). At the beginning, his brain rhythms were very asymmetrical, with peaks of 3 microvolts at 9.0 to 10.5 Hz and 20 to 33 Hz, and 2 microvolt peaks between 3 and 5 Hz. During the meditation, the brain rhythms became symmetrical at 10.5 to 12 Hz, with an occasional 10-microvolt peak at 9.0 Hz. The beta rhythm remained asymmetrical,

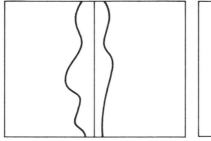

At the start

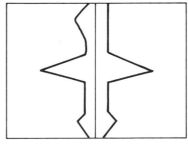

During Meditation

and in general the patterns were rarely over a 3-microvolts peak at any frequency.

He reported a very happy feeling in the end, though in the beginning, he did not know that he was going to meditate, so that he was a little embarrassed beforehand.

HARRY SMITH

This subject was not connected to the EEG. He commenced with a skin resistance of 325 kilohms per centimeter squared, which increased during Divine Love Devotion to 950 kilohms per centimeter squared (65% relaxation response). He had not learned any meditation system before. During Divine Love Devotion, he had a feeling of no thoughts, yet there was also a feeling of happiness within. He "felt some spiritual energy coming from the outside and entering into his heart." He felt that he was swaying with joy.

MRS. ROBERTS

This woman had never meditated before and was rather nervous. She was not connected to the EEG. Her skin resistance changed from 450 kilohms per centimeter squared to 800 kilohms per centimeter squared during the Divine Love Devotion (43% relaxation response). At the beginning, she felt disturbed and wanted to escape, saying she "was aware of stuff within myself rising up." Later, she felt very comfortable.

PANDYA

An Indian gentleman who observes his ritual formalities but has never meditated before in a systematic way. "I felt in the beginning a dark cloud," he said; then during the meditation, the darkness was gone and he saw a faint light of dark blue color. He had a very happy feeling during meditation and felt tears in his eyes. This was the first time he had had such an experience. His skin resistance changed from 1.5 megohms to 1.75 megohms (16% relaxation response). He was not connected to EEG.

LIONEL OSWALD

A student training to be a barrister, who has been meditating for six weeks under the guidance of Swami Prakashanand. He produced very symmetrical brain-rhythm patterns of 10 to 20 microvolts amplitude at 10.5 Hz together with 3- to 5-microvolt peaks at 4.5 and 19 Hz, and maintained this rhythm throughout the meditation. He felt "too involved with the instruments to do well," but nevertheless showed an excellent pattern.

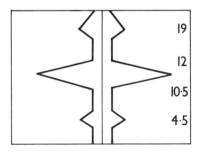

BARBARA SANDOWN

A Yoga teacher and healer with previous experience of many different kinds of meditation over a number of years. During Divine Love Devotion, she felt a strong energy coming into her body and spreading all over, then felt disembodied and became a part of the chanting. When the swami touched her hand, muscular tension decreased markedly and alpha activity at 9.0 Hz increased over the 10-microvolt level, while responses at 4.5 and 19 Hz were maintained. Skin resistance began at 550 kilohms per centimeter squared and increased to 2.5 megohms per centimeter squared (relaxation response of 78%). Throughout meditation, she had a feeling of someone sitting at her side.

ISABEL CADE

Has been meditating for about seven years, using a variety of methods. Initially she showed rather erratic rhythms (inferior to her usual patterns), slowly showing alpha-theta. Skin resistance fell from 200 kilohms per square centimeter to 100 kilohms per square centimeter. When Swami-ji touched her head, patterns instantly shifted to state-five consciousness with weak delta and theta but strong (5–6 microvolts) alpha. The patterns began to randomize later, and Swami-ji again placed his hand on her head, this time producing a stronger state-five pattern, which persisted to the end of the session. The subject just "felt comfortable" until touched by the swami, then began to lose her body boundaries and to "become part of the chanting," with feelings of bright light and exotic fragrance. Subsequently, she had slightly euphoric feelings for a day or two, with hallucinations of Swami-ji being nearby. This settled down to a feeling of increased

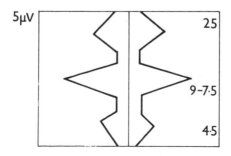

calmness and confidence. At the end of Divine Love Devotion, her skin resistance had risen to almost 400 kilohms per square centimeter (relaxation response of 50%).

JOHANNA JONES

Throughout the first session, she showed a steady decrease in skin resistance, but eventually (in the second session), she showed a relaxation response of about 40 percent. She reported "not much" from the first session, but during the second Divine Love Devotion, had "a feeling from when I was much younger." Then she reported a sensation of being "like a ball or sphere; full-up; felt lopsided, one side of me taller" (subjective correlates of stage-four relaxation response). Her brain rhythms were asymmetrical in the first session, but became more symmetrical later.

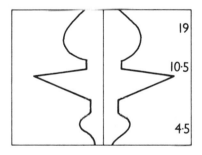

GEOFFREY BLUNDELL

Many years experience of meditation of different traditions. During Divine Love Devotion, he became "aware of hearing through the heart."

Comments on the Brain Rhythms of Swami Prakashanand Saraswati

The swami was wired up to the Mind Mirror at the commencement of the afternoon, and the brain rhythms were examined at intervals. The rhythms were, he said, his ordinary waking state all the time. They were a weak (5 microvolt) state-five consciousness.

Summary and Conclusions

We have had the opportunity to examine the brain rhythms of several persons experiencing Divine Love Meditation and of monitoring the skin resistance and verbal reports of others. There is evidence for both temporary and, in some cases, long-term elevation of the level of consciousness even after a mere twenty minutes of this practice.

Some Traditions of Meditation

ZEN

Zen is wonderfully, sometimes almost painfully, down-to-earth. A Zen story tells how a young monk went to his master full of excitement and said, "Master! Last night, during meditation, the Buddha appeared to me in a great cloud of

light. And again, this morning, the same marvelous vision!"
The master replied: "Return to your meditation. Pay close attention to your breathing. The visions will go away." For
Zen, perhaps more than any other tradition, is not concerned
with spiritual delights. It is in ordinary everyday life, full of
human error, suffering and misery, that Zen hopes to realize
Nirvana—the end of suffering, the end of sin. Zen aims at
equanimity of mind, no matter what the upheavals of actual
existence.

The meditation of Zen is called Zazen, which simply
means "sitting in Zen." Sitting in Zen means just sitting, not
hoping to become a Buddha (Zenists would call that lack of
concentration and lack of sincerity), not trying to become
anything, just being.

The beginner in Zazen is instructed to pay passive attention to his breathing, not trying to control it, not comment-
ing upon it, just being aware of it without thinking of it, lest
that should inflate the ego, the I, the me. He is simply,
quietly aware that breathing is going on. To help him keep
his mind on his breathing, he counts his breaths. It is not
that the breathing is all that important, but it all helps to
keep his mind from external things. The counting begins
with an out-breath, "one." Successive outbreaths are counted
until the tenth. Then the counting begins all over again at
one. Some masters amplify the instructions for beginners by
telling them to imagine a deep well beginning inside the
head and running into the ground beneath them. As they
exhale each breath, they mentally toss a coin into the well
and watch it slowly sink to the bottom. This continues until
there is a little pile of ten coins at the bottom of the well;
then the procedure starts all over again at one.

Sooner or later the pupil will find that the counting is
becoming confused and that this may be followed by one of
two things: he may awaken suddenly with a feeling not so

much of having fallen asleep as of just not being for a while. Or he may suddenly become aware of being aware, of being acutely aware of everything going on in and around him, with at the same time a sense of profound detachment or even rightness about everything. Now he is really beginning to be able to just sit.

In terms of modern neuropsychology, he is becoming able to be aware of his own perceptions, of his own right-hemisphere operations. Sights, sounds, smells, dreams, reveries—the whole content of his personal unconscious (to use Jung's term) is displayed before him, and he witnesses it all without either choosing any particular content or hanging onto one when a new content begins to enter the field of awareness.

Now we begin to understand why the physiological correlates of Zazen are those of a very wide awake mind combined with those of a profoundly relaxed body.

Unfortunately, to the Western world, the phrase "a wide-awake mind" has misleading connotations. The expression summons up images of thinking, scheming, planning or avidly seizing upon every sense impression in case it signifies the need for action. To the Zenist, a wide-awake mind is something like a perfect mirror: it reflects everything, missing not the smallest detail, but holds nothing.

Zen has no sacred literature of its own and treats the sacred literature of Buddhism as so much waste paper. Zen insists upon individual inner spiritual experience, which is mainly to be acquired by the practice of Zazen. Zen claims to be the very innermost essence of Buddhism, directly transmitted by Buddha himself to his greatest disciple, Mahakasyapa, although there are no historical records of this transmission. Legend has it that once, when the Buddha was seated with his disciples, Mahakasyapa approached him, offering him a golden flower and asking him to preach. Buddha accepted the flower and, holding it up, looked at it silently. After a time, Mahakasyapa smiled, for he had become enlightened.

In our experience, the two physiological changes which accompany Zazen are a shift of the EEG pattern to low-frequency alpha (about 8 Hz) plus steady theta at about 4.5 Hz and an increase in skin resistance of five to six hundred percent. It is an alert but profoundly relaxed state.

TRANSCENDENTAL MEDITATION

The practice of Transcendental Meditation, or TM, centers around the repetition of a mantra—in fact, for most practitioners, the mantra is the whole of TM—so we must begin by considering what *mantra* means. Early in the Vedic Age of India (a period of from roughly 2500 B.C. to 700 B.C.), the Hindus discovered that sound vibrations can have a profound effect upon the emotions. Just a poem, a song or a piece of music can affect one's mood, so the Indians came to recognize that particular sounds could facilitate states of deep meditation. These special sounds are termed *mantras*, and they consist of one word or sometimes of several words or even a series of sanskrit letters.

One-syllable mantras are called bija mantras, or seed mantras, the most famous of these being OM (pronounced A-U-M). The number of mantras is unknown, but there is a physical limit to the variety of sounds which can be produced by the human voice, and most of these are common to all languages. In Hinduism, each sound has its proper expression in some object, so that everything in the universe has its own particular sound, which is its natural name.

The Maharishi Mahesh Yogi brought TM into the world. He was born at Jabalpur, Central India, in 1913, and studied at Allahabad University, where he obtained a degree in physics. During this period, he met his guru, His Divinity Swami

Brahamananda Saraswati (1869–1953), who had spent most of his adult life as a solitary monk. The maharishi became one of the special pupils of Swami Saraswati, who taught him the technique and meaning of TM.

After Swami Brahamananda's death, the maharishi spent two years as a solitary hermit and then began to hand on Brahamananda's teaching. Eventually, in 1957, he founded the Spiritual Regeneration Movement with the aim of spiritually regenerating the whole world.

In TM, each pupil is given a special mantra which is supposed to be psychologically appropriate to his or her temperament. The mantra is not to be disclosed to other people but practiced in private. However, since only a finite number of suitable mantras is possible, many people use the same mantra. Robbins and Fisher in their book about TM, *Tranquillity Without Pills* (1972), say: "In our cases, the assigned mantras have worked well, but we believe that we might have obtained the same results by using any of the many mantras that are in use."

The maharishi himself says, "Each man meditates on a given word, suitable to the impulses of the man. The sound of the word is important, not the meaning, but the quality of the sound." Over and over again, the maharishi insists that TM is almost effortless, that there is no religious involvement and that no change in the pupil's life-style is required other than sitting in meditation twice daily. He says: "It does not need a long time of silent meditation to reach Transcendent Being; just a dive within the self for a few minutes and the mind is infused with the nature of pure consciousness which keeps it enriched through all the activities of the day. This is the way to live the spiritual life."

Our observations, both with experienced TM practicers and with our own pupils trained in the use of mantras, is that the physiological correlates are very similar to those which accompany Zazen, that is, symmetrical, low-frequency alpha and theta rhythms, together with an increase in skin resistance of five to six hundred percent (the Omega 1 ESR reading falls from 25 to somewhere between 3 and 5).

THE YOGIC MEDITATIONS OF PATANJALI

There is no doubt concerning the historical existence of Patanjali, but there is some controversy as to his identity. Some scholars attribute the famous Yoga Aphorisms to a Patanjali who lived somewhere around 300 A.D. Other authorities believe he was Patanjali the grammarian, who lived in the second century B.C. Fortunately, it is agreed that whoever Patanjali was, he did not invent or develop the techniques about which he wrote so eloquently, but rather systematized and recorded knowledge that was already several thousand years old.

Patanjali begins with the statement that "Yoga is controlling the activities of mind." As long as the mind restlessly flits from one thing to another, one identifies oneself with mere sense-objects. Only when the mind is completely withdrawn from sense-objects and concepts can it identify with itself. The very first requirement, if we are to lift ourselves up from the low condition in which most people permit their minds to dwell, is to control the flow of ideas in the mind. Patanjali goes on to say that there are five kinds of ideas, some painful, others pleasurable: right knowledge, wrong knowledge, delusion, sleep and recollections.

The implications are enormous. If we really do automatically categorize every idea immediately as it arises, and then proceed upon the assumption that our categorizing was correct, any error could be disastrous. If we mistake delusions or dreams for knowledge of reality, or if we confuse recollections with here-and-now perceptions, then we are confused and on the path to becoming mad.

We must now turn more specifically to the yogic traditions concerning practical methods for gaining mind control. It is in the last three "limbs" of the eight limbs of Yoga (the eight necessary practices) that we find the following clearly defined states of mind:

concentration—*dharana*
meditation—*dhyana*
contemplation—*samadhi*

In the first of these, concentration, attention is focused upon one particular idea or object unwaveringly. Yogis like to point out that without a certain amount of concentration, a person would hardly be able to live at all and certainly would be unable to work effectively at any kind of task. It follows that most individuals get some training in *dharana* in the course of everyday life. In *dhyana*, there is a play of thought upon the object of attention and its associations. The mind considers every aspect of the object that is known or can be inferred but is not permitted to stray to other matters. Thus if the object is a burning candle (a popular object for formal meditation), the size and shape of the wax column is considered, then its color and probable weight. The outer and inner flame are noted, the wisp of smoke and the pool of molten wax below the flame. Where and how the candle was manufactured, how long it will burn and even "candles I have known" may be considered. In contemplation, the third "limb," one must forget oneself entirely and permit the candle to become the only thing of which one is aware—there is only the candle; there is no self to contemplate it.

Concentration, meditation and contemplation form a

closely connected series. Concentration, being a sensory-perceptual functioning of the brain, is a right-hemisphere exercise. On the other hand, meditation, defined as a logical, analytical, abstracting and associational functioning, is a left-hemisphere exercise. Contemplation, wherein all sense of self is lost, with only a vague memory of some vast, ineffable experience perhaps remaining subsequently, seems to be related more to what Jung meant by the "transcendental function."

Another of Patanjali's exercises can be interpreted for the modern Westerner as follows:

1. Sit quietly in the correct posture (spine erect and not leaning against anything) and pay attention to anything going on in or around yourself. After a little while, begin to label all the sounds and vibrations—airplane overhead, rain on the windows, vacuum cleaner downstairs, heavy truck going by, police siren.

2. After practicing 1. for ten minutes or so, change your attitude of mind and try to respond to every sound as if you had never heard anything like it before.

This can be a most revealing exercise. In 1., the left hemisphere is employed in one of its favorite activities: categorizing. In 2., there is noncritical, nonanalyzing awareness. This will often bring us to a startlingly clear understanding of how much information we normally suppress by selective inattention to stimuli.

Our observations have shown that only very experienced yogic meditators achieve profound relaxation with the threefold exercise of *dharana, dhyana* and *samadhi*. More usually, an ESR change of two hundred to three hundred percent occurs (the Omega 1 reading falls to somewhere between 8 and 12). In the first two phases of the meditation (*dharana* and *dhyana*), the EEG patterns is that of alpha blocking, but in the third phase, very experienced practitioners produce the state-five pattern.

THE MEDITATION OF GAUTAMA BUDDHA

Hardly any other part of the Buddha's teaching is as thoroughly misunderstood as what he has to say concerning meditation. The word *meditation* is understood in the West to mean "to plan mentally, to design, to ponder, to cogitate," and is misunderstood as escaping from the world into fantasy, religious contemplation or some kind of mystical trance. Hardly anything could be further from the Buddha's teaching.

The original word used by Buddha was *bhavana*, which means "development" or "culture," so that the proper interpretation of the Buddhist *bhavana* is "mind development." The object is not dissimilar to Patanjali's aims: to cleanse the mind of lustful desires, indolence, restlessness, ill will and illusions, and to cultivate instead such laudable qualities as concentration, living in the here and now, openness to life and experience, tranquillity and awareness.

Before his enlightenment, Buddha studied yogic methods under various contemporary teachers and is said to have attained the highest states of awareness that these practices could provide, but he felt that these states were just euphoric experiences which gave no insight into the nature of ultimate reality. They were, perhaps, states comparable to what we today term sixth level or seventh level (active creativity and psychedelia), as contrasted with the illuminative level, or cosmic consciousness. Buddha therefore developed Insight Meditation, intended to take the practitioner to the fully illuminated state. The *bhavana* of Buddha is compounded of observation, vigilance and acute self-awareness.

One of the most important forms of *bhavana* is that which has become one of the cornerstones of Zen: being acutely aware of everything one does, physically or verbally, throughout the whole of the day. Whether one gets up or lies in bed, whether one dresses or undresses, whether one talks or keeps silent, eats or drinks—in these activities and in all others, one must be fully aware and mindful of what one is doing here and now. Live in the present moment, live in the present action: that is *bhavana*. There is no need to practice any special exercise in order to practice Buddhist mindfulness; one is simply mindful and aware of whatever one does.

Another aspect of *bhavana* is that of analytical awareness of all our thoughts and feelings. When one feels unhappy, depressed or miserable, one must examine the causes and find out how the feeling arises, not in an attitude of criticizing but in a scientific spirit of inquiry.

Exercises

1. Mindfulness. Sit down in the evening and mentally go back to when you awakened in the morning. Now try to recall the whole of the day's events in their correct order. As far as possible, do not give yourself a verbal account ("then I put on my left shoe and tied the lace") but let the events unfold in a pictorial form as if they had been filmed. If you come to a time for which you just cannot remember what you were doing, note it carefully before going on through the day. If, on the other hand, you find that your mind has drifted away from the events of the day onto any other subject, go back to when you arose and start the day all over again. Try to recall not only every event but your own feelings

in relation to each event. At the end of the exercise, note carefully how many occasions there were for which you had no recall, or only partial recall, of what happened.

2. One-Pointedness. Listen to the sound which can be heard within your own dominant ear (is it the left ear or the right?). See if you can clearly focus upon this internal sound, which is often similar to the sounds heard in a seashell or to a high-pitched whistle almost beyond audible range. Concentration must be absolute throughout the exercise.

3. One-Pointedness. Listen to a musical record or cassette and gradually lose the idea of "Here I am, listening to music and trying to concentrate." Try not to let the music bring back images or pictures which are the result of past associations, and avoid critical analyses like, "This is a poor recording," "This is not a good arrangement." When your ego, your I, your ordinary, everyday critical self (i e., your left-hemisphere consciousness) becomes completely absorbed in the flow of sound, you will find your consciousness beginning to expand, as well as wider and wider significance in the musical experience.

4. Facing Yourself. To what extent, in all honesty, are you held back by the Five Hindrances—lustful desires . . . ill will, hatred or anger . . . torpor, langor and laziness . . . restlessness and worry . . . sceptical doubts? Try not to be self-censuring, just honestly analytical.

5. Mindfulness of Breathing. Just be aware and mindful of the movement of your breathing. Do not attempt to impose control over your breathing and do not struggle against any attempt to impose such control. Any effort arouses the fight-or-flight response and destroys the relaxation response. Do not think, "I am being aware of

my breathing." This centers on the I instead of on the breathing and makes you more self-conscious. Just be aware of breathing going on.

6. Meditation upon the Four Sublime States.

  a. Extend unlimited, universal love to all living beings without discrimination of any kind.

  b. Radiate compassion for all living beings who are suffering, in trouble or with an affliction of any kind.

  c. Radiate sympathetic joy in others' successes, welfare and happiness.

  d. Meditate upon the importance of maintaining equanimity in all vicissitudes of life.

The Mindfulness of Breathing exercise is similar to Zazen, and it is perhaps not surprising that the physiological correlates of experienced students are the same as those found with Zazen.* The two exercises on one-pointedness described above produce, in our experience, results similar to Patanjali's meditation on a candle but with deeper relaxation (Omega 1 reading between 5 and 9) and often showing much stronger alpha waves in the EEG pattern.

THE RAINBOW

You are calm and relaxed, awake and aware. There are no images in your mind, no words floating inside your head.

---

* There is considerable person-to-person variation in the physiological correlates, and our observations support the age-old claim that attitude of mind is more important than technique. Exercises like the Meditations on the Four Sublime States produce wide variations of response (except with advanced meditators, who show state-five EEG patterns), and their main interest of the scientific observer is in the left brain–right brain variations shown.

All is at rest. All is at peace. . . . Now your consciousness begins to move into another reality . . . you are walking along a country path, very conscious of the sun on your face and the light breeze on your cheeks, and the song of birds all around you. Where does this path lead? You wonder about this, but almost as soon as the question forms, you know that you have been here before. Now there are more branches of trees overhanging the path; it is darker; and yet your certainty of knowing what is in front of you increases. It is a beautiful afternoon, and you have a wonderful sense of security and peace.

For some minutes, you have been aware, without really noticing it, of a faint rushing sound originating somewhere in front of you, and abruptly you come upon the source. A magnificent waterfall, shimmering in the brilliant sunshine, suddenly becomes visible as you come upon a large, open clearing in the midst of the trees. You gaze enraptured by this unanticipated vision of beauty; the breeze causes fine clouds of iridescent spray to dance around the fall as it cascades into the pool below.

You stand still, absorbed by the beautiful view; feeling the warmth of the sun on your head and allowing the rays to flow through you, invigorating you through and through. The sound of the waterfall also seems to flow through you, penetrating and soothing every cell in your body. As you stand in the woodland clearing, it seems as though there were a voice . . . Now you hear it more clearly: "Be still," it says, and obeying this inner voice, you allow yourself to become still, no longer directing your attention, no longer trying to control anything at all, but *being,* and being aware of the whole scene around you.

As you gaze at the waterfall, you smile, because a lovely rainbow can be faintly seen in the mist. As you watch, it becomes more intense, its brilliance seeming in some strange way to be related to your stillness. As your stillness grows, it seems to communicate itself to everything around you; you even gain the impression that the waterfall is ceasing to flow. Not that there is any less water cascading down, but rather that the movement is being captured in some dimension which is paradoxically outside time. You continue to watch, motionless, and minute by minute, you realize that your time is no longer that of the world around you. Your heart beats in the same steady rhythm . . . your breathing has the same steady ebb and flow . . . but a hurrying bee is moving more and more slowly; a swooping hawk seems just to be floating down . . .

Something very odd is happening to time. Everything around you is slowing down more and more; the movements of all living things have slowed right down, and the gay songs of the birds have become sad dirges as the pitch of the notes falls lower and lower. The whirling, twisting, cascading shapes of the waterfall seem to suggest eternal movement by their very stillness. The rushing sound of the water has completely died away and the quietness has flowed through every rock, every tree, every branch and leaf, and every blade of grass. Leaves that were falling from the branches hang suspended in mid-air, their flight to earth halted by the cessation of time. The stillness has even permeated the river, now frozen into curiously angry shapes at the foot of the fall, and into smoother undulations along its further reaches as it disappears from view among the still, silent trees at the far side of the clearing. The whole unearthly scene still radiates the friendly warmth of a lazy summer afternoon: you feel the warmth pouring down from the motionless sun.

Now that time has ceased to be, you no longer have to be still, for you and the stillness have become one. You wonder what would happen to that magical stillness if you actually moved, and so you slowly advance one foot. Nothing changes, and so you move the other foot with more confidence. Nothing changes, and in a flash of illumination, you realize it is because your inner stillness has remained intact. What an incredible experience it is! Like being in a three-dimensional picture, captured at the moment you began to be still. You reach out to a leaf on a nearby bush, touching it very carefully, for you feel it might be as fragile as gossamer, for all its living appearance.

Following the path behind the waterfall, you now walk right up to the crystal curtain which was the water itself. Earlier, you would have been beaten to the rocky floor by the weight and power of the torrent, but now, though still majestic, it is strangely tame—controlled by your stillness. You run your hand over the smooth, twisting forms, and then over the rougher edges of the frozen spray. For a while, you stand in contemplation of this living sculpture, realizing how much of nature's exquisite art normally goes unperceived.

You move on to the foot of the rainbow, half-dazzled by its scintillating colors and yet longing for their healing touch. You experience a blissful feeling as if you were being taken up into the rainbow—or is the rainbow being taken up into you? The deep glowing colors seem to penetrate your body, each seeking its own destination. The red light seems to have an affinity with the base of your spine and to bring with it a robust feeling of the life force itself. The orange rays, merging with your lower abdomen, convey a sense of the joy and fruitfulness of life. The yellow light seeks its home just below the navel, bringing with it a sense of life's exultant triumph over inanimate forces. With a complete change of mood, the green radiance caresses your heart and somehow makes you think of the deeper meaning of life, those spiritual things that lift man above mere biological existence. The blue light, coming to your throat, and the indigo, centering between your eyebrows, bring you an understanding of destiny and of your part in it, and of the spiritual powers needed to play that part. The purple seems to move and tremble in the crown of your head, arousing a strange sensation as of a beautiful flower opening its thousand petals and somehow uniting you with the Spirit of the Universe . . .

There seems to be a play of colors up and down your spine . . . You have the feeling of vista upon vista of things inexpressible rising up before you, of boundless possibilities, of seeing into the farthest distances . . . The colors dance and weave into a tunnel of light seemingly proceeding from the heart of the universe. You have a feeling of being swiftly and smoothly borne through that tunnel toward a boundless ocean of peace and strength . . . Suddenly the voice speaks again, saying: "Remember these things, and remember me. I am your inner Stillness."

MEDITATION

A *bhikku* went to the Zen Master and said: "Master, I am worried.

Speak to us of meditation."

And the Zen Master replied, saying:

"You live in a world which is hypnotized by the illusion of time,

A world in which the so-called present moment is seen as nothing

But an infinitesimal hairline dividing an all-powerful causative Past

From a fascinatingly important and alluring Future.

But you have no present moment.

Your consciousness is fully occupied with memories on the one hand

And with expectations on the other.

Cannot you comprehend that there never was, is, or will be,

Any experience other than the Present Experience?

You are therefore out of touch with reality

And live in a world of illusions.

You meditate when you attend, without attachment, to the Here and Now,

When your unfocused mind is aware, without comment, of whatever Is.

You meditate when, without ceasing to be conscious of your body and your mind,

And of the clamoring voices of your environment, you become increasingly

Attuned to the Voice of the Silence, to the Wisdom of your Higher Self.

You meditate when, in the quietness of the Woods and Fields,

Or in the peace of some old Church,

You turn inward for a while to share the Stillness of God.

Yet you meditate more worthily when in the thick of Life's battlefield,

In the heart and dust and strife of the daily round,

You carry with you that same Stillness

So that your heart becomes the Temple of your Spirit.

You meditate when you live neither wholly in this world nor in that,

When you steep your mind in the waters of divine creativity and intelligence,

And your every act is redeemed by being taken up

into something greater than itself.

You meditate when, in the agony of indecision, you say,

"Not my will, God, but thy Will be done."

But you meditate most of all when you listen—

With the ear of your body and the ear of your mind and
the ear of your soul—

To that soundless Voice that speaks from the eternal
cosmos

And bids you be One with all of Life.

THE PYRAMID
(Geoffrey Blundell)

You are calm and relaxed, very alert but relaxed. There
are no images in your mind, no words floating around inside your head. You are aware of a movement but you do
not yet know what it is. Now it is clear, you are part of a
camel caravan which is traveling across the desert, part of
a pilgrimage to the most sacred sanctuary in the world.
Hour by hour, the journey continues, the hot sun pouring
down on this unreal, sandy landscape. On and on, over
dune after dune, the sandy surface rippled by the wind
into static waves. You are protected from the worst of the
heat by your white *jellaba,* which holds a layer of cool air
around your body.

    You cannot reach your destination before the evening,
and so you abandon yourself to the awkward rhythm of
the camel's movement. Now a wave of anticipation
arouses your fellow travelers, for in the distance, just on
the horizon, can be seen the tip of a large building. You
stare at your goal, which seems to now vanish in the shimmering heat of the desert sand, and you wonder if it is yet
another mirage . . . But no, soon much more of the edi-
fice can be seen, and it is indeed the sacred pyramid toward which you have been journeying for many weeks.

A little while later, there you are in front of this magnificent structure, one of the seven wonders of the world, the largest temple that you have ever seen. Now you are at the entrance to the most sacred part of the pyramid and you suddenly have a vision of the future, when for many thousands of years, this entrance will be sealed and the sacred purpose of this pyramid forgotten.

You enter the passageway, which slopes gently upward, holding onto the person in front of you, for you can see nothing after the bright glare of the sun. Soon your eyes are used to the gloom and you can see tolerably well in the light of the wax tapers. You are surprised at how fresh the air is, and you understand that there must be a complex system of ventilation to carry away the smoke from the tapers.

You begin to climb many steps, up and up and up. After a while, you lose count of the steps, as higher and ever higher you climb. You seem now to be separated from your fellow travelers, yet you hardly notice, for your awed excitement at your nearness to the sacred source. At last, you enter a great hall high up in the pyramid, and this hall, itself in the shape of a pyramid, is lit by more tapers. These tapers, though, are barely visible against the shaft of sunlight which falls onto a throne in the middle of the hall. This is the moment for which you have been preparing—you know that you will now mount the throne.

On the throne, you feel that you are being drawn up the shaft of light; even so, you know that the person you have always been is still seated on the throne. This is the moment you have heard so vividly described in ancient philosophies, which until now you could hardly visualize, as you rise into that greater entity which is you. You will never again feel frightened at the possible loss of that small ego which remains on the throne, and from this level, you regard very tolerantly and very lovingly the little foibles and weaknesses of that smaller aspect of yourself which came to make this pilgrimage.

You reflect to that small person on the throne the certainty, which you will always remember, that death will not cause you to disappear like a drop of water in the ocean, but rather will expand you into a greater purpose, a growing through of level after level as you fulfill a divine design.

To the one seated on the throne, you project an image of how you would like to be. For a moment or two, visualize as clearly as you can—no words in your mind—that ideal self which you would like to be. That self who is more healthy, who more often follows his creative impulses, whoever your ideal self may be.

Now allow that image to flow into the figure being held in the light on the throne. As this ideal image enters the pilgrim who is you, let your consciousness return there also, bringing with it a deep understanding of these revelations. Know that in the future, in times of greatest difficulty, you can call on this experience of a higher consciousness—now and always.

THREE
Biofeedback and the Healing State

Chapter 8

Mind-Mirror Research with Well-Known Healers

It was the recognition of the frequency-triad pattern in the classroom experiments that first suggested that a thorough examination of the brain-wave patterns in healers and their patients might prove fruitful.

In order not to risk developmental forcing, we took care that healers, as subjects, were not given training for fifth-state consciousness until they had shown their ability to attain it spontaneously during or after meditation periods.

In our initial tests with healers, it was quickly apparent that there was some difference between the first appearance of the beta-alpha-theta triad in the meditative, quietly seated condition and the ability to hold this pattern of brain activity while fully active, and also some suggestion that in the fully active condition, the specific rhythms could be of slightly higher frequency.

For example, in experiments with Mr. Edgar Chase, Mrs. Rose Gladden and Major Bruce MacManaway, three notable healers whose healing is frequently of a very active type (that is to say, they often move their hands a good deal, or talk to the patient during the healing session), it has been noted that the beta rhythm in particular tends to be nearer to 25 to 30 Hertz than the 16 to 18 Hertz first observed in classroom subjects (in other words, they are more aroused).

In a privately circulated report on tests done a month earlier with Mrs. Addie Raeburn, a healer with many clients from the medical profession who acknowledges limitations to orthodox medicine, we had recorded:

> Within a minute of attending to the subject, Mrs. Raeburn begins to produce both alpha and theta brain waves; the alpha being continuous and the theta initially intermittent but becoming continuous within five or six minutes. These brain rhythms become disturbed, but do not cease, even when she talks to the subject or to observers.
>
> Simultaneous ESR measurements show an increase in skin resistance of about 150 percent (60% relaxation) within two or three minutes of commencement. This depth remains sensibly constant until she arouses at the end of the session. At the end of a session, skin resistance rapidly returns to normal, theta may persist for half a minute or so, and alpha persists for several minutes (even with eyes open and talking).
>
> Subjects almost invariably go into a trance the maximum depth of which is related to (a) their trance experience; (b) the severity of their illness. Whereas Mrs. Raeburn's trance is typical of autohypnosis or meditation, subjects show varied states, such as "somnambulism" in which theta brain rhythm is accompanied by an ESR showing hyperarousal. Frequently, the depth of a subject's trance varies in inverse ratio to the distance from the subject of Mrs. Raeburn's hands. At other times, the subject's ESR is seen to vary synchronously with that of the healer and in the same sense.

When we reexamined Mrs. Raeburn with a pair of matched EEGs, noting every frequency which the instruments would register, we found that both the healer and her patients almost invariably showed the frequency triad (alpha-beta-theta) during the healing process. Later, we found that various different healers began to show the triad shortly after the commencement of a healing session, and the patients then began, more slowly, to develop the same pattern. Usually, during the healing process, the patient's EEG pattern showed a slow but fairly marked increase in amplitude, while the healer's pattern showed a corresponding amplitude decrease. Both patterns returned to normal within five to ten minutes at the end of the session.

When the Mind Mirror became available to us in 1976, our original intention in applying it to the healing situation was to look for objective evidence of any peculiar "healing rhythms" in either healer or patient or any interaction between the brain states of healer and patient.

All this evidence was rapidly forthcoming, but the unexpected bonus came when we were monitoring Mrs. Raeburn and a patient who had received very extensive leg injuries in a bomb accident.

The work of the surgeon had been remarkable, and with regular weekly healing from Mrs. Raeburn, the leg was almost completely restored although there was some residual loss of function, and the man could not balance on one leg or ride a bicycle.

During the healing session, it was observed that although the healer was showing fifth-state brain rhythms, the patient was showing a very ordinary unilateral pattern. Since healing was being carried out with the healer's hands at the legs, we suggested that the hands might be moved to the patient's head instead.

Within twenty-five minutes of the change, the patient was

showing the bilateral fifth-state pattern. Of greater importance, within three days, the residual disability had cleared up—the patient could maintain good balance as well as ride a bicycle.

Further experiments have shown, in confirmation of that early discovery, that varying the position of the healer's hands (for those who employ the "laying-on-of-hands" technique), even without the patient being aware of the change, not only alters the patient's brain rhythm but also his level of arousal as shown on the skin resistance meter.

This was the stroke of serendipity by which we stumbled upon the principle of biofeedback healing, using the instrumentation of biofeedback to help a healer deploy his skill to the maximum advantage, and in subsequent work with some thirty or so prominent British healers, we have uncovered so much more of significance that the entire question of nonmedical healing seems, at last, open to detailed scientific study.

It is not the object of our inquiry to evaluate the phenomenon of healers per se (it would be impossible, in any case, since they are of such diverse form and background) or to assess their many varied beliefs, which may range from believing themselves to be channels for divine energy (with a profoundly religious feeling) to believing that they give of their own vital or "magnetic" force (regarding this as a biological phenomenon), to that they bring about "healing rapport" as some kind of physical or psychological interpersonal relationship which facilitates the patient's self-healing, to that the healing emanates from discarnate entities for whom they act as the medium.

All these, as well as any other beliefs and philosophies they might have, appear to be compatible with the possession of demonstrable healing ability. If, however, healing power is related to higher states of consciousness, there is a psychological component, an attitude of mind that seems to emerge as a common denominator. Healers generally show an acceptance of that which is invisible, a high tolerance for unrealistic experience of that which is related to the mystical, and in their dealings with people, of openness to life and experience, of readiness to meet things more than halfway, of dissolving the wall between themselves and other people, the usual me/you, we/them, mine/thine divisions.

The effective healers have, if not compassionate love, great empathy, as well as the ability to still their minds, to be calm and undisturbed, to extinguish their personal egos and become part of something they feel is higher than themselves.

Quite clearly, it is almost impossible to define a "healer" in satisfactory scientific terms. For even when the healer is demonstrably successful, many medical people will point to the possibility that the healings were spontaneous remissions or attribute them to earlier medical treatment with a delayed effect.

It may be pertinent to recall here the conditions laid down by Pope Benedict XIV for a cure to be considered a miracle:

1. The disease must be serious and impossible, or at least very difficult, to cure.

2. The disease must not have reached a stage at which it was liable to clear up spontaneously.

3. No medical treatment must have been given, or if any were, it must beyond doubt have been ineffectual.

4. The cure must be instantaneous or nearly so.

5. The cure must be complete.

6. The cure must not be preceded by any crisis due to natural causes at the expected times.

7. There must be no relapse.

Apart from the fact that Pope Benedict required a cure to fulfill all these conditions *simultaneously* to count as a miracle, it is clear that most of the conditions are very difficult to be sure about individually.

Our criteria are easier. We are happy if the healer can, in a single healing session of from several minutes to one hour (because healers differ enormously in their time requirements), produce alleviation of pain and discomfort and an apparent improvement in the patient's condition which is sustained for a substantial time.

Objectively, we look for a *normalization* (not, specifically, an increase or a decrease) of the level of activity of the sympathetic nervous system, as shown by measurement of electrodermal resistance.

We also look for an increase in nervous-system response to challenge, that is to say, the ability of the nervous system to respond to environmental change.

Finally, we look for a decrease in the time needed for the level of nervous-system activity to return to normal after a stimulus, which is tantamount to a reduction in anxiety level. A simple skin-resistance meter gives all those measures in a minute or two. After a successful healing session, a patient will be more relaxed yet at the same time more wide awake and better able to respond to emergencies. These physiological changes seem to be the result of the healer inducing in the patient one or both of two responses, namely, deep psychophysiological relaxation and fifth-state consciousness.

The important factor is that bilateral symmetry of brain function seems to be central to health control in general. We find that people at the top of their professions, no matter what they may be, tend to have more symmetrical patterns. Healers, like Yogis, Swamis and Zen Masters (we speak of these later) have exceptionally symmetrical patterns, and the power of the healer seems to be related to the amplitude, symmetry and stability of his patterns. The stability seems to be the most obviously related factor, but it is closely dependent on the other two.

For the past ten months, we have been privileged to work with Major Bruce MacManaway and his colleagues during his regular visits to London. Here, by being able to join in the clinical situation and following cases right through to cure, we have been able to learn a great deal about the practical deployment of healing ability.

Some of Major MacManaway's assistants are strong natural healers with little practical experience, and we have been able to demonstrate how, by using instruments to monitor the patient's brain responses, they can learn to deploy their powers to maximum effect. It has become abundantly clear that, for the great majority of healers, it is essential to keep the attention focused upon the job of healing. Contrary to the belief of some healers, permitting the attention to wander from one thing to another and even speaking to the patient may not only result in a reduction or loss of the healer's fifth-state EEG pattern, but in loss of the patient's healing pattern also. Sometimes, as shown by the instrument check on the nervous-system responses at the end of the session, there is a loss of healing effects, too. Because of the exceptional facilities offered by his clinic and the tireless cooperation of Major MacManaway himself, we have even been able to establish that the loss of healing effect which occurs when the healer's attention wanders is, to a first approximation, proportional to the weakening of the healer's fifth-state EEG pattern.

Those healers who, like Major MacManaway, Edgar Chase and Rose Gladden, can maintain full healing effect while interacting freely with the everyday working world are those in whom the fifth state is fully developed. It follows from this that for those healers who find it difficult to be fully effective in everyday working conditions, a well-tried remedy is available—meditation. Many studies apart from our own (those at the Maharishi European Research University, for example) have shown that meditation greatly increases the bilateral symmetry of the brain rhythms.

In another area of work with Major MacManaway, we have also tested the effect on the Mind Mirror of up to six or seven healers standing behind a patient. We find that as each of the healers joins the team, the amplitude of the patient's fifth-state pattern increases. This bears out Major Mac-Manaway's own theory that the healing energy, whatever it may be, is intensified by the working together of more than one healer and of groups of healers.

We have also carried out tests on "absent" healing. Our question was whether the healer and the one to be healed both have to be in close proximity in order for healing to take place.

To ascertain whether a patient's brain rhythms, and therefore his Mind Mirror patterns, could be affected at a distance, we conducted an experiment with Edgar and Hilda Chase, both well-known healers.

Edgar Chase left the consulting room and went into another room, where he was connected to a Mind Mirror, while the patient remained with Mrs. Chase (both of whom were connected to Mind Mirrors), who pretended to be getting ready to commence healing. An arrangement had been made whereby as the clock struck the hour, Edgar Chase would begin absent healing. Geoffrey Blundell was with Edgar Chase to witness his Mind Mirror and ESR responses, while Maxwell Cade and his wife remained with Hilda Chase. With the striking of the clock, Geoffrey Blundell observed Edgar Chase's patterns immediately change to state five, while the patient in the consulting room suddenly showed the same pattern about fifteen seconds later, and stayed in this condition for ten minutes.

While such an experiment on an isolated occasion proves nothing by itself, does this evidence imply that absent healing is more likely to occur when the "sender" is in fifth state, whether or not the healer knows he or she is in it? And does the patient's fifth state, responding to the healer's, create in him or her the climate of healing, in other words, the harmonization of both brain hemispheres together with the triad of brain-wave rhythms that harmonizes the nervous system and allows the body to heal itself? We have thought the result sufficiently impressive to justify the series of more stringent tests which have now been set up.

Digressing a moment from the Mind Mirror to another example of how healing ability can be channeled into a most effective clinical form, we cite again the work of the healer Edgar Chase. A former physicist, Edgar Chase has always been in the habit of keeping meticulous case histories, and for nearly a year now, he has been using biofeedback instrumentation as well. We quote some brief extracts from a report he recently sent.

I am using an Omega One Skin Resistance Meter applied to the left hand of the patient. A second instrument is connected to my own left hand, my right hand being the positive hand which channels the power. Remarkable results have been obtained. A patient is immediately responsive to the healing power and when the healer's hand is held over the cerebellum an increase in arousal is shown.

In all seriously ill patients and particularly those on tranquillizers, arousal is low—the basal resistance readings of such people being usually abnormally high. *There is evidence of severe tension in most seriously ill patients.* The first treatment is to eliminate tensions by treating specific acupuncture points in the back, shoulders and neck of the patient. Within 5 minutes the nervous tension shows a reduction of from 40% to 80%.

At this point, and only then, treatment of the basic problem can commence. The response of the patient to direct treatment of his problem is accelerated significantly when he is completely relaxed. Migraine can disappear in 5 minutes as opposed to an hour . . . An asthmatic attack disappears completely in 20 minutes. The instrument records all changes and is a valid key to the monitoring of progress . . .

Not to be overlooked in this brief digression, we would like to mention the often crucial evidence of excessively high ESR combined with lack of response to stimulus (usually six deep breaths) as a warning that potential illness is present even to the imminence of a cold. In one particular case, in 1974, a student in our classes, a young woman in her early thirties who is a probation officer, feels she owes her life to the clue she received through a very low-current reading (indicating high ESR) on her meter, combined with a complete lack of response to the hyperventilation test.

We indicated to her that this could mean the presence of a systemic disease and urged her to seek a medical opinion. Fortunately, she followed our advice. As a result, the trouble was diagnosed as cancer of the cervix. She had two operations and was told she had caught it just in time.

The Family Planning Clinic to which she had gone for her tests was puzzled that she would want another smear after having had a previous one with negative results. They humored her, and when the result was positive, she did not explain her grounds for suspicion; having been a nurse herself, she felt it might complicate the issue. But she was not surprised.

I knew that when everyone else's machine was going up, and mine just dropped down, that something must be very wrong. I also felt extremely tired, although there were no other apparent symptoms. I don't know why I thought it might be a gynecological problem: it was just a hunch. I only know there was a point when I was doing very badly in the hospital and both my husband and I thought I might not make it. Needless to say, Max put me in the hands of a healing group, and somehow I felt the help I was getting.

This student has not only recovered but has gone on with classes and has learned to maintain the fifth state and do healing work for others. She has become very creative and even hopes to become a teacher in our work.

One of the highlights of our research experiments with healers and the Mind Mirror took place at the Wrekin Trust Sixth Annual Health and Healing Conference at Loughborough University last year, when Rose Gladden agreed to demonstrate our fifth-state pattern during healing before an audience of some four hundred doctors, scientists, psychologists, healers and laymen on closed circuit television.

Rose Gladden was connected to one of the machines, and Nora Forbes, wife of a doctor, volunteered to be connected to a second one to receive a healing.

For a matter of twenty minutes or so, the entire audience was able actually to watch on the screen the brain waves of the healer form into the colored-light pattern and transfer to the subject. Not only that, but the successive stages of the healer's inner state—relaxing first, and then steadily falling into the altered state of consciousness—were clearly shown. Within a very few minutes, Rose Gladden was producing the strong alpha waves, and then gradually Nora Forbes relaxed into them, too. After about fifteen minutes, both healer and patient appeared to be completely attuned.

It was such a clear-cut and undeniable demonstration, in terms understandable and convincing to all, that the audience was stunned. People cried; one or two even sobbed.

Rose Gladden explained what she had felt and experienced. "I tuned in to a large golden cloud and channeled this love through my heart and hands to Nora." She felt that there seemed to be something wrong with Nora on her left side, below the ribs.

Later, Nora Forbes, who had panicked initially by facing such a large audience, ended up feeling very deeply relaxed and refreshed and admitted that she did have a kidney problem. She believed that the session had been very helpful.

This demonstration signified an important breakthrough in our research, for it went beyond the need to describe and explain and train to that which could be seen by one and all.

One point which we must emphasize here is the importance of the healer's own health, both physical and mental. Even a common cold can reduce a healer's effectiveness, and mental depression can temporarily deprive him of healing power. But what appears to be an occupational hazard of present-day healers is exhaustion from sheer overwork. Healers are dedicated people, and the numbers requiring their help are endless. It all too often happens that one finds a tired and harassed healer struggling to cope with an endless list of patients, but refusing to admit that anything is wrong.

During a series of weekly studies of Mrs. Raeburn, we observed a gradual falling-off of the strength of the healer's EEG pattern *associated with a weakening of the pattern induced in the patient.* Mrs. Raeburn is an exceptionally alert and responsive person, so as soon as these observations were brought to her attention, she took a holiday. On her return three weeks later, she showed a complete recovery of the strength of her own EEG pattern, and a corresponding increase was shown in the patients' patterns.

Since then, we have observed the same effect in numerous healers, including two more of the most prominent names, and have seen evidence that this can be a serious hazard. We have seen powerful healers who, after eight or nine weeks of continuous work, were not only unable to induce the usual ESR and EEG responses in their patients, but seemed to "heal in reverse."

In these cases, as the healing session progressed, the healer's weak EEG patterns became stronger while the patients' patterns became weaker. Moreover, not only did the patients' ESR measurements at the end of the session fail to show the expected improvement, but the patients themselves sometimes volunteered the information that "they didn't seem to get so much out of it this time."

Clearly, it is part of the healer's ethical responsibility to keep a watch on his own health and not to overwork to the point where the healing session becomes a mere outer form devoid of content.

An important corollary of healing research has been to extend it to our students to ascertain whether those who achieve the fifth-state pattern are potential healers. We have for the past few months brought the test for healing ability into the classroom, and to test for healing ability with the hundred or so students we have trained to produce full fifth-state consciousness, we introduce the same healer-subject situation with the Mind Mirror as we use with established healers.

So far, out of this hundred, we have found about fifteen students who met the requirements, that is, the transfer of the pattern to the subject, with the resulting harmonizing of the subject's nervous system and benefits of health, sometimes to be seen at once, as cure, sometimes as a process of improvement. Our aim is to continue to develop methods for the effective training of people to realize fully their innate healing ability and to apply it to the maximum benefit of the patient.

The production of healing ability is not, however, the same thing as producing healers. We have already found that numerous persons of undoubted healing ability are not effective healers because of faulty technique, lack of necessary precautions or slipshod organization.

To this end, we are giving an Introductory Course for Healers, covering elementary anatomy and physiology together with practical instruction in healing and measurement of the trainee's ESR and EEG patterns, which eventually will culminate in the award of a Certificate of Competence to successful candidates. We will work with healing organizations and trainers in healing generally, and through this comprehensive instruction, hope to raise the general standard of healing and to enhance the status of healers in the public eye.

Looking back, we see we have come a long way from our first modest goal, which was to test a few healers for our own enlightenment; but now many healers are coming to us for theirs. It turns out to be a two-way search for further revelation of what has always been totally mysterious. For a *feeling* of healing, no matter on what basis of belief, can be seen to have a physiologically measurable correlate—it provides that subjective feeling with supportive objective evidence. If, further, that objective evidence turns out to be the ultimate criterion of healing effectiveness, then there is very substantial promise in its development.

It has been pointed out many times and in many ways that we are all potential healers and that undiscovered healers are all around us, everywhere. Despite wide disagreement with this premise, this also applies to the medical profession, where more and more doctors are becoming interested in healing, particularly in its relation to biofeedback monitoring. For, if a medical man can utilize healing ability as well, there is no limit to what can be accomplished for the health of humanity.

In this context, we would like to tell of a doctor who

approached us at a conference and asked to be put on the Mind Mirror to see whether he had potential healing ability. We were unhappy to learn that his rhythms were those of an ordinary academic (mainly beta). Fortunately, we thought of something we could try before telling him the bad news. We asked him to imagine that he had a patient in his office for whom he could do little or nothing by conventional medicine. We then asked him to attempt to heal this patient, relying solely on pure compassion. Almost immediately, the brain waves began to change, and in a minute or two, his pattern was that of a strong healer.

During the course of our work with healers, our fifth-state research opened up for us with another visit of Swami Prakashanand Saraswati, who wished to be tested in this regard.

His brain rhythms, except when he deliberately relaxed into mindlessness, were those of a powerful healer, with the difference that not even Rose Gladden, who has the most stable and imperturbable rhythms that we have yet seen in any healer, could match the unwavering stability of the swami's pattern. Nor have we seen anyone who could equal the swami's feat of touching a number of subjects on the head and immediately raising their pattern of consciousness by two levels—from the ordinary waking state into the advanced fifth state. In at least one of these subjects, the higher state persisted for three days and was an unforgettable experience.

On another occasion, the swami certainly illustrated the principle of the Awakened Mind when he produced the most beautiful fifth-state pattern on the Mind Mirror for more than an hour while engaging in an intense debate with Professor John Hasted, a noted physicist.

The swami was intrigued and fascinated with this technological demonstration of the long duration of his inner state. He maintains that every step up the ladder of consciousness brings one nearer to God consciousness and that God consciousness contains all powers.

Our research with other teachers and adepts, whether of Transcendental Meditation, Yoga, Zen or any other tradition, have strongly suggested that meditation, so long as it is practiced correctly and regularly, does indeed progressively change the individual's brain patterns to a more bilaterally symmetrical form, which is then carried on, as a higher state of consciousness, into daily life.

In conclusion, we should perhaps point out that at present, there is no existing guide to the kind and prevalence of EEG patterns which can be found in a cross-section of the population at large. Also, there is no published material illustrative of the course of events which typically occur during EEG biofeedback training, and that our work in this field has therefore been very much of a pioneer exploration.

Nevertheless, we feel that our biometric studies have already proved to be of great value in relation to the higher states and healing.

Chapter 9

The Role of the Fifth State in Long-Term Clinical Healing

We rarely see patients privately unless they have at least completed the Basic Course in classes. We believe that difficulties with interpersonal relations play an important role in most psychosomatic illness and that group therapy therefore serves a double purpose. If a subject who has completed the course still wishes and needs private counseling, or if a patient is referred directly by a hospital or general practitioner, we still proceed on the principle that the long-term resolution of personality difficulties that enables the individual to take control of his or her own problems is more important than the short-term removal of symptoms.

Deep psychophysiological relaxation (DPR) is just as effective as hypnotherapy in producing almost miraculous relief of symptoms. But, unless the subject has had training in self-control of internal states, the first time he finds himself in a stressful situation similar to that which precipitated his original symptoms, they will return. Biofeedback training is not so open to this criticism. Specific biofeedback training without general training in becoming a more relaxed person *may* produce only a temporary improvement (e.g., frontalis muscle training for relief of tension headaches), but if it is combined with general biofeedback measures, it can be a very effective means of effecting permanent cures.

Examination of the EEG patterns of patients is a routine procedure; it shows clearly that the long-term effectiveness of any therapy is related to the bilateral symmetry of brain rhythms and to the patient's ability to attain the state-five pattern at least during relaxed and meditative periods.

To illustrate this higher-state element and its vital importance, we give a few case histories from our files:

DR. NANETTE CLIFFORD
Age 45. General Medical Practitioner.
COMPLAINT: Intractable back pain, especially in the lumbar region, severe enough to interfere seriously with her work. Chain smoking and increasing side effects from the drugs used in attempts to control pain. Dr. Clifford had completed both parts of the Basic Course before informing Maxwell Cade that she had a two-and-a-half-year history of arthritis and had recently been compelled by side effects to reduce her analgesic intake to the point where they were no longer effective. She had found the course effective in helping her cope with stress and even to reduce smoking but now needed assistance in applying what she had learned to the control of pain.

Examination showed a great deal of tension in the back and in the trapezius muscles. In the first private session, she was given one hour of training in EEG alpha-wave production, followed by practice on a particular meditation theme which she had found effective and which, on this occasion, enabled her to reach 80 percent relaxation.

At the second session, one week later, Dr. Clifford reported that she had been able to reduce her intake of drugs by fifty percent, with decreased pain. She also felt much better able to cope and had been practicing her meditation regularly. No alpha training was given this time (EEG patterns were strong and symmetrical), but there was a one-hour led meditation during which she attained 90 percent electrometric trance for more than fifty minutes. She later felt euphoric and was free of pain for a whole day.

At the third session (again, one week later), Dr. Clifford was obviously improving. Her drug intake had now been cut by 75 percent, but she had been unable to give up smoking completely. She was repeatedly tested on her capacity for autoinduction of trance states and, by a variety of methods, was able to attain levels of 65 to 78 percent relaxation in three to five minutes. In a led meditation sequence, she rapidly reached 94 percent relaxation.

Of more importance than any of the foregoing, she volunteered the information that she realized that her improvement would only be maintained if she could keep the meditative calmness with her all the time, and she felt that with her increased self-awareness, this would now be possible.

The fourth session showed continued improvement, with a reduction in smoking and further reduction in the use of analgesics. She felt fully able to cope and was altogether more optimistic. Six months later, she reported that the improvements were fully maintained.

MRS. I. HERMES
Age 48. Company director.
COMPLAINT: Agoraphobia (fear of going out among people) since the death of her husband some four years ago.

Over the last eighteen months, this had become acute, but she had been frightened to seek advice until a friend introduced her to Maxwell Cade's classes. The classical phobic picture was present: rapid breathing, sweating, trembling, muscular tension, dryness of the mouth. She was unable to walk about in public without an escort. When she attempted to leave home unaccompanied, she experienced a feeling that something terrible was about to happen. She had experienced several panic attacks, during which she feared that she was about to die from a heart attack.

During the first three sessions, her EEG and ESR readings were so irregular that it was difficult to obtain meaningful data until deep relaxation had been induced (by a combination of alpha-frequency strobe lighting and comforting word pictures). While deeply relaxed, she was given suggestions of increasing self-confidence, better interpersonal relations, emotional calmness and being wanted by her friends and associates. By the end of the third session, she had been able to reach 92 percent relaxation and had spontaneously recalled a number of emotional situations related to interpersonal difficulties. During the fourth session, she relaxed to 90 percent without any tremors or hesitation, and after almost three hours, awakened in a permanently more relaxed state (ESR had increased from around 200 kilohms/cm.sq. to 750 kilohms/cm.sq.). Despite the nervous system improvement and subsequent subjective feelings of better health and energy, there was still little improvement in her agoraphobia.

During the seventh session, her ESR indicated a strong spontaneous arousal, and on arousing her and gently questioning her about this, she exclaimed: "I can't get people out of my mind!" This related to business acquaintances, and discussion led on to other situations of an interpersonal nature. She had one small group of friends with whom she felt really comfortable, and was asked to examine the difference *in her own attitude* toward this group and toward others. This resulted in an insight into the part played by her own attitude in her difficulties. She was then desensitized by being asked to fantasize increasingly more frightening agoraphobic situations, returning to the company of her really comfortable friends in between the exercises. Ten days later, she telephoned to say that she had been out shopping on her own for the first time. After twelve sessions (spread over 18 months), she is now able to resume her attendance at European trade fairs and conferences, completely free from her former fears. She has resumed our classes, and is also attending Yoga classes, "To widen my circle of friends," she explains.

MISS G. MASON
Age 43. Film producer.
COMPLAINT: Extreme anxiety, insomnia, chain smoking, feelings of inadequacy. Miss Mason had completed both parts of the Basic Course and a course of Methods of Meditation before saying, "There's something I'm missing out on— I don't seem to let go properly." She was extremely frightened of letting go, and little progress was made in the first two sessions. There were various words used in the led meditations which she found highly disturbing without knowing why, and these had to be changed so that she could be deeply relaxed (and also listed, so that each word could later be used as an approach to her history). Her insomnia cleared up in five sessions (by which time her ESR and EEG patterns were showing her improved relaxation), but Maxwell Cade made no attempt to deal directly with the smoking until, after seven sessions, all resistance to profound states of relaxation had been removed. Since her doctor had advised her to stop smoking, it was important that this be handled effectively. She was given suggestions such as, "Of course, you will decide to

stop smoking one day," for several sessions before this was eventually changed to "You will decide to stop smoking next weekend." Miss Mason never ceased to be amazed at the ease with which she dropped the habit and the lack of any temptation to start again. At the tenth session, she reported:

> Oh, things, are so much better now! I can go to different places now and mix with all the people I have to with practically no anxiety. I used to worry myself silly wondering whether I'd done or said the wrong thing. My attitude to people has changed a lot. I used to be able to put on a bold front, but now I feel easier with them and I'm really beginning to enjoy myself.

After seventeen sessions spread over twenty months, all her difficulties have vanished. She continues to hold down an exceedingly demanding job, but without any sign of stress or overtiredness.

MISS L. ERICKSON

Age 28. Business executive.

COMPLAINT: General tension, insomnia, sinusitis, catarrh and skin rashes, extreme fear of flying. "The trouble is," said Miss Erickson at the first session, "I've just been offered a fabulous promotion. But it means touring all around Europe and I'm absolutely terrified of flying!" The symptoms were classical. Sinusitis, catarrh and skin rashes are almost the distinguishing marks of the psychosomatic subject, while insomnia characterizes the chronic worrier. The EEG was very revealing, showing strong, well-defined theta, alpha and beta on the left side, while the right showed only incoherent electrical noise. This suggested the possibility of suppression of dreams and fantasy, which was confirmed by the patient's own account. She had obtained a good honors degree at college and thought she owed it to her family to make the most of her intellect. She remembered few dreams, those which she did recall being mainly of a nightmare quality.

Notwithstanding her bright intellect, Miss Erickson did not realize the close connection between her different symptoms. She thought of herself as a mess, full of excuses for not getting on with life. This was quite untrue. She was, in fact, very hard-driving and, far from being lazy, she was overtired.

Insomnia is one of the most common complaints. Lack of sleep produces a vicious circle which embraces depression, depleted energy, inability to cope and a worsening of anxiety, which disturbs sleep still more. The successful treatment of insomnia depends upon reducing the underlying anxiety. Sleep is not, as many people believe, a complete release from the cares and efforts of daily existence and the enjoyment of mindless bliss. It is rather a period of relaxation not far from the conscious level which can readily be disturbed by a wide variety of stimuli, including our own thoughts, emotions and worries. The ability to enjoy sound sleep depends largely upon the degree to which the individual can shut out unwanted stimuli.

At the first session, Miss Erickson was asked to fill in a Manifest Anxiety Questionnaire consisting of seventy-five questions about personal attitudes, preferences and behavior which are closely related to anxiety level. The result (moderately high anxiety) agreed well with her ESR measurement (250 kilohms/cm.sq.). Because of her high intelligence, it was possible to discuss the meaning of this with her and to explain how all the symptoms could be alleviated by reducing the basic anxiety level. She was then asked to imagine that she was in a taxi on the way to Heathrow Airport. Sweat ran down her face as she experienced the terror of the imminent flight. Then she was thoroughly relaxed by a combination of pleasant word pictures and Schultz Autogenic Exercises (page 76). She was then asked to imagine arriving at the airport and going through customs. This time the anxiety level was appreciably lower.

Miss Erickson had four sessions in two weeks because of an impending flight to Brussels with two business colleagues who were also friends of some years' standing. She was taught autogenic relaxation as well as a mantra and was given fifteen minutes of strobe relaxation at each session (the flashing red light was set at seven flashes per second, the alpha/theta border frequency). Even before the flight, her insomnia was less of a problem. When she returned from Brussels, after experiencing no more than minimal tension both ways, her insomnia cleared up and did not return.

She had six further sessions every two weeks before going on an extended business trip to America. During this period, she was helped to relive some early, highly emotional experiences and to reassess them herself from an adult viewpoint. Training in myographic relaxation of frontalis muscles and in alpha/theta production was also given.

A year later, Miss Erickson introduced a friend to the classes and at the same time reported on her continued progress. None of the original symptoms had persisted, although she frankly admitted that she still tended to push herself too hard. She meditated regularly, practiced autogenic exercises when she found she was getting tense and somehow coped with an amazing work load. She believed that a large part of the secret was getting above it all. "I try as much as possible to bring the meditative attitude into all the everyday things," she said. "Sometimes I don't do very well. I even forget or fail to make time for my meditation for two or three days until I realize that I'm getting the old sense of strain back. But I do try especially to keep my interpersonal relations right."

MR. I. MACKINTOSH

Age 55. Managing director.

COMPLAINT: Agoraphobia, depression, gastritis, fear of death. At the first visit, the patient was accompanied by (or, rather, brought by) one of his executives. He was unable to drive his car and frightened to be alone, and immediately launched into an account of his fears. His doctor insisted that there was nothing wrong with him and had told him to pull himself together, which only increased his fears. He was incoherent and unable to give any material from which a case history could be constructed. He was, however, an excellent hypnotic subject and was soon able to put himself into a state in which he readily followed further suggestions of relaxation. After the session, he felt good and was eager to fix the next appointment. He was given autogenic training at the next two sessions, together with guided fantasies. After the third session, he said, "I felt as if I had a head and no body. . . . Do you know, I've had a lovely dream—for the first time in many years. Oh, that *was* nice." Previously, he was too frightened to be wired up to the EEG, but at the fifth session, it was possible to ascertain that the right-hemisphere rhythms were much weaker than the left and that he required much relaxing before he could produce any alpha at all. At the sixth session, he could produce long trains of high-amplitude alpha, and his relaxation began to improve rapidly. At the eighth session, he arrived on his own, having driven thirty miles down the highway without any fear. He began for the first time to speak openly about marital difficulties and other interpersonal problems, and to express a keen interest in the inner meaning of meditation.

As he seemed ready for the step, he was instructed in one or two simple forms of meditation. A cassette tape recording was made so that he could practice at home, and this soon began to show results. By the twelfth session, he could produce continuous alpha and theta on the EEG and regularly reached 90 percent relaxation as shown by his ESR. His fear of death had vanished. He took up control of his company again (which had been delegated for almost two years), and began once more to enjoy golf and other social activities. Gastritis and some depression persisted until the fourteenth session (spread over five months), by which time he was fully active and, according to his friends and colleagues, looked ten years younger. He attributed his recovery mainly to learning to meditate, to being able to retire from the everyday, often frenetic world into the beauty of his own inward world, to being able to face difficulties (and he had many genuine difficulties) with calmness, tolerance and courage.

MR. R. M. VERNON
Age 62. Judge.
COMPLAINT: Several years ago, after a life relatively free from illness of any kind, he broke an ankle badly in a skiing accident. There were also "greenstick" fractures of the leg bones. From the time of the accident onward, the leg was never free from severe pain. Eventually he began to suffer side effects from the drugs used to alleviate the pain and, on the advice of a specialist, agreed to have the leg amputated below the knee. After the operation, the pain in the phantom limb was worse than ever. He was unable to work and began to suffer liver damage from the drugs. He was first seen about eight months after the operation. No proper ESR measurements could be obtained because of the effects of the drugs.

He had, however, four natural advantages: a kindly and tolerant personality, very high intelligence, an experience of travel in many parts of the world and the ability to visualize vividly the places he had visited.

At the first session, it became apparent that he had all the qualities of the psychosomatic health syndrome and only needed a technique for the control of pain. He was hypnotized and maintained deep trance for an hour, and after he had become completely relaxed, was instructed how to produce profound relaxation by vivid sensory images. He was also instructed in autogenic relaxation methods. On the way home in the chauffeur-driven car, he slept for an hour and a half—"The best sleep I have had for many months," he said.

At the next two sessions, he was again given deep relaxation followed by instruction in a variety of meditation methods. At the fourth session, he arrived unaccompanied, having driven the car himself ("For the first time in a very long while!" he said). He could now relax himself at will and control the pain with little difficulty. At the fifth visit (only six weeks after the first one), he was beginning to show normal responses on the ESR, had resumed his duties and was beginning to enjoy life again.

MR. R. STOCKPORT
Age 36. Business Executive.
COMPLAINT: Shaking hands. Bad enough to be a social embarrassment. The habitual slopping of drinks over the nearest person tended to disappear or be markedly reduced when he was on vacation but to become severe in stressful interpersonal situations. Surprisingly, the shaking hands were not accompanied by insomnia, skin rashes, sinusitis, gastritis or any of the other frequent accompaniments of anxiety states. He did, however, have very cold hands—another characteristic of the anxious patient—which warmed up 18

degrees F. during autogenic relaxation! His ESR showed only moderate hyperarousal, while his EEG pattern was excellent—a weak but nicely symmetrical state five. His posture suggested muscular tension, and he was found on examination to have very tense trapezius muscles. He was a bright, intelligent person who took a very lively interest in the biofeedback machines. After the second session, he was given a tape cassette of the autogenic sequences for practice at home. During the third session, while in a profoundly relaxed state, he recounted the origin of his trouble in a highly emotional situation some six years earlier. His production and control of brain rhythms was good enough for him to be able to watch the Mind Mirror patterns with his eyes open and to direct them consciously. He related best to the myograph monitoring the tension of the forehead muscles; in fact, he became so good at this that he was loaned a monitor myograph for practice at home. The first setback came when he took an overseas holiday and was separated from biofeedback equipment and taped-relaxation sequences for three weeks. Early in the first week, he experienced some embarrassment in a social situation. There was some hand trembling, and he became afraid of being unable to control it. Then he became still more afraid that his drinking, which originated in an effort to reduce tension and had only been overcome with his success in biofeedback relaxation, would again take control. This started a downward spiral of increased anxiety, more trembling and more anxiety.

Fortunately, when he resumed treatment, he regained full control inside a fortnight. He suffered from a certain amount of shyness, and our discussions with Mr. Stockport were aimed at boosting his self-confidence. After ten sessions (covering a period of six months), he was not drinking, not taking tranquilizers, reported greatly improved interpersonal relations and appeared to be quite capable of looking after himself in the future but has not yet been completely weaned from the biofeedback machines.

MRS. G. SAINTON
Age 68. Secretary.

COMPLAINT: Tinnitus (ringing noises in the ears) of about eight years' duration, completely unresponsive to medical treatment. General anxiety. This woman, with her doctor's approval, was about to fly to California for a six-month course of biofeedback treatment when she heard from her osteopath that treatment was available in London. Through her daughter, who lives in California, the lady arranged for full details of the treatment given by the American clinic to be made available to Maxwell Cade. The treatment was based upon myographic relaxation of the frontalis (forehead) muscles, which almost invariably produces relaxation of the neck and scalp muscles as well.

The tinnitus was exceedingly severe, causing her acute misery, crying and prostration. In the first session, the patient was given both the recommended myographic relaxation and EEG alpha/theta biofeedback training, together with a Mind Mirror examination. The right side of the scalp had much more muscular tension than the left, corresponding to the more severe tinnitus in the right ear. Overall relaxation (as shown by ESR) was twice as good with EEG biofeedback as with EMG biofeedback, and her Mind Mirror rhythms when she was thoroughly relaxed were those of a weak state five. The session included thirty minutes of guided imagery and a brief (4 minutes) session on the alpha strobe light.

At the second session one week later, she reported greatly

improved sleep (tinnitus used to wake her up several times in the night) and that "I feel better in myself."

The second session included full training in the Schultz autogenics sequence (which were tape recorded for her home use) and several brief guided fantasies (also recorded). At the third session, she reported three periods of more than one hour during the day with no tinnitus at all (for the first time in more than five years) and no interruption of sleep at night. At the fourth session, she reported marked improvement in the tinnitus, at times not even bad enough to cause real distress "except when my friends took me to an exhibition which I didn't really want to go to." Her osteopath had commented on the marked reduction in tension in her neck and shoulders. One whole day had been completely free from the awful noise in her ears. She was now given a second tape for home use, this one a blend of gentle music and guided fantasies which had proved to be particularly relaxing for her. At the fifth session, she said, "I'm changing! Little things don't worry me anymore." During this session, there was a brief but violent thunderstorm, of which she professed to have been very frightened since childhood. She remained perfectly relaxed throughout. In the week preceding her sixth session, she "had a very harassing time which just didn't let up. The tinnitus became really bad at times, but often I could control it by deliberately relaxing." At the seventh session, she reported continued general improvement and added, "Also, I don't have the nightmares I often used to have."

Here is Mrs. Sainton's *Tinnitus Diary* for the first few weeks. She was asked to rate the severity of the noise on a scale of from one to ten, four times a day (7 A.M., 11 A.M., 3 P.M., and 7 P.M.) and to record the weekly average for each time of day.

The foregoing table shows clearly the woman's impression

Tinnitus Diary

	7 A.M.	11 A.M.	3 P.M.	7 P.M.
Week 1	6.9	5.3	4.7	3.3
Week 2	5.4	3.6	3.0	3.0
Week 3	5.0	3.3	1.5	1.1
Week 4	5.0	3.3	1.5	1.1
Week 5	2.8	1.7	1.3	2.0
Week 6	2.0	1.4	2.0	1.0
Week 7	2.2	2.0	1.1	1.1
Week 8	2.0	1.3	0.7	1.3
Week 9	1.3	1.1	1.6	1.1
Week 10	1.2	1.2	1.4	1.4
Week 11	1.2	1.2	0.04	1.0
Week 12	1.3	0.9	0.7	1.0
Week 13	1.0	1.1	0.7	0.5

of how much the noise had abated in the first three months of her treatment. The figures were corroborated by the myograph records, which showed how much her forehead muscle tension had been reduced, and by the Mind Mirror patterns, which showed a corresponding improvement in the bilateral symmetry and amplitude of her EEG patterns.

At this point, her attendances were reduced to once a fortnight, and rather more time at each session was spent in explaining to her the extent to which she owed improvement in symptoms to her own changed attitude to life. She had gone from being a timidly complaining pessimist to a tough-minded optimist, and she clearly realized this, once it was pointed out to her. The following extracts from her *Tinnitus Diary* show how the improvement continued. The very low figures are due to the high proportion of days in which she experienced no tinnitus at all. She had also completely given up even occasional use of sleeping pills or tranquillizers:

Tinnitus Diary

	7 A.M.	11 A.M.	3 P.M.	7 P.M.
Week 23	0.6	0.4	0.1	0.4
Week 27	0.3	0.4	0.3	nil
Week 31	0.5	0.3	nil	nil
Week 35	0.07	0.07	nil	nil

Her friends tell her she looks years younger. She herself says, "My life has been totally rebuilt."

Chapter 10

Implications
and Future Trends:
A Commentary
by C. Maxwell Cade

The subject of this book has its roots in the ancient East; its growth and expansion in the West is very recent. In fact, it is only in the last twenty years that we have had our attention increasingly drawn to the physical and mental benefits which can be obtained from allied practices such as Schultz's Autogenic Training, Jacobson's Progressive Relaxation, yoga, meditation and, most recently, biofeedback. Even the thoroughly "respectable" and reputable scientific and medical journals are reflecting this interest.

Perhaps most widespread of all these new or rediscovered ways to personal growth is meditation, but many of those who join the large movements manage to maintain the association for years without attaining any clear understanding. They approach the subject—as we all do—with their own preconceptions and expectations. Often they are given minimal training in some form of concentration exercises, with no explanation of the psychological or physiological principles involved and little guidance as to the transpersonal aims.

According to the cultural bias of the individual, the practice which they have been taught may be regarded as a system for aiding the spontaneous development of his own deepest potential, as a panacea for all physical illness, as an alternative to conventional religions or as a way of escape from the difficult problems of daily life.

On the other hand, many people are afraid to really yield themselves to meditation because of the possibility that they may become alienated from their business affairs, hobbies or day-to-day interests, or they may even dread to enter the unknown regions of their inner beings for fear of what they might find that has been guarded and repressed.

In spite of the plentiful information now readily available concerning most meditation practices, one factor that the Western mind needs is missing, that is, any hint as to the unifying principle which underlies the multiplicity of techniques. The interested student may read about Buddhist meditation, the meditation of Saint John of the Cross, Zazen, Tibetan tantra and a host of others, and he may feel that at some level, there must be a common denominator.

Frequently, schools within each of the great traditions make claims to being the one true way, and there is little evidence that there has ever been a serious effort to establish even the similarities in psychological and physiological effects, let alone to search for a common root in all traditions. We have to thank the Maharishi Mahesh Yogi for stimulating the interest of modern scientific investigators like Dr. Keith Wallace and Dr. Herbert Benson, who have done so much to establish the reality of the physical benefits of meditation.

Whereas nearly all the scientific work on meditation and other forms of yoga has been carried out by psychologists or physicians, who had obtained their degrees years before they even heard of these practices, my own interest in making a scientific study arose because I was introduced to meditation years before I studied psychology or physiology.

It just happened that one of my school friends was a Japanese boy, Rio Shimizu, who aroused my interest in judo, kendo, Zen and other esoterica, and through his father introduced me to the *Budokwai* (the Ways of Knighthood Society). At about the same time, a doctor-friend of my father's who was coaching me with my swimming also imparted to me much of his knowledge and enthusiasm for Gurdjieff, Ouspensky and others, as well as Sufism in general. It was he who first introduced me to the strange idea that I was not properly awake, that I suffered from selective inattention so that I only noticed the things I wanted to notice, and to the fact that most people suffer from the terrible disease of non-stop, automatic, mechanical production of words for the sheer sake of talking. I found it all very difficult to understand.

But in this accidental manner, I acquired a little knowledge of both Zen and Sufism (and some of their remarkable similarities) six or seven years before I went to medical school, where I began to learn scientific incredulity, and to wonder whether my beloved studies of esoterica were some passing madness. All Eastern ideas, I found, were treated with scorn and derision, so I began to keep my interests strictly to myself for fear of being ostracized by even my closest friends, so different was the climate of opinion forty years ago. I began to understand, too, why my father, who had studied yoga, was so secretive about it, though I had been brought up on a diet of the Kim Game (looking for just one minute at a table covered with pencils, knives, notebooks, pepper pots, paperweights, cotton spools and other everyday articles, and then making an accurate drawing and descriptive list of the whole thing), and long walks during which I had to breathe in for six paces, hold my breath for ten paces, breathe out for four paces, and so on. I started this at a very early age, and it all seemed quite natural!

After the Second World War, at the request of Gunji Koizumi, the great Japanese teacher to whom I owe so much, I became for a while a member of the committee which first formulated proposals for a British Judo Association. At that time, I was much concerned with teaching methods, both in relation to judo and to Raja Yoga, having founded a small club. Then my job (I was an experimental officer in the Royal Naval Scientific Service) took me away from London, and I founded another small group in which I tried to develop teaching methods, but with relatively little success.

Another ten years went by until, in 1963, the New York Academy of Sciences invited me to visit America—not in relation to Eastern arts, but because of my current job of experimental cancer detection. In Philadelphia, I became involved in the setting up of the first large-scale breast-screening clinic, and also became acquainted with a whole range of electromedical equipment which was almost unheard-of in Great Britain.

Seven years later, it dawned on me that biofeedback equipment provided both the ideal way to teach meditation and relaxation and also provided a means for investigating the psychological and physiological effects of different traditions on a comparative basis.

Not that the relaxation response, which is what biofeedback instrumentation most readily enables us to measure, is the whole, or even the main part of meditation. But it is the common entry path to all altered states of consciousness except the ecstatic. Biofeedback instruments have enabled me to achieve a thirty-year-old dream: to be able to teach the basic elements of different techniques of meditation (including a full, conscious awareness of every bodily change as it occurs) in two to three months, as compared with the years which it took in my day, and still does at many schools. (Something I had utterly underestimated is the inquisitiveness of the Western mind. I had never imagined how fascinated Western pupils would be by the physiological approach to meditation, and how Westerners would love to record their arousal level, nervous-system responsiveness and resistance to stress!)

For meditation and allied arts to have their full effect in producing a more humane and elevated society, however, it will have to become far more widely accepted than it is today, and many cherished materialistic attitudes will have to change first. For although science has advanced enormously since the time of Darwin (1809–1882) or of Haeckel (1834–1919), the doctrine of evolution is still accepted, and so until very recently was Haeckel's notion of the human brain and mind, that is to say, that the living brain and the mind or soul are a unity: the mind or soul is an epiphenomenon of the functions of the brain. And it is less than a century since the distinguished scientist Emil Du Bois-Reymond in 1880 delivered to the Liebnitz session of the Berlin Academy of Sciences his famous speech in which he propounded seven enigmas of his time:

1. the nature of matter and energy
2. the origin of physical motion
3. the origin of life
4. the seemingly preordained orderliness of nature
5. the origin of sensation and of consciousness
6. the origin of rational thought and of speech
7. the problem of free will

Problems 5. and 6. can be seen to relate to the development of the right and left hemispheres of the brain, respectively. Emil Du Bois-Reymond considered 1., 2. and 5. to be of a different order from the other enigmas. The problem of consciousness was one of those which he thought was utterly transcendent and insoluble.

Intermediate between the materialism of the nineteenth century and the intelligence-came-first attitude of modern humanistic psychology is that of Sir Arthur Eddington, who, in his 1929 Swarthmore lecture said:

> In comparing the certainty of things spiritual and things temporal, let us not forget this—Mind is the first and most direct thing in our experience; all else is remote inference.
>
> Picture first consciousness as a bundle of sense-impressions and nothing more. . . . But picture again consciousness, not this time as a bundle of sense-impressions, but as we intimately know it, responsible, aspiring, yearning, doubting, originating in itself such impulses as those which urge the scientist on his quest for truth.

My own feeling is that we will have to improve our general level of awareness quite a lot before we can really appreciate what a benefit the East-West, ancient-modern synthesis of self-awareness and self-control will be for humanity. We live too much in a world of sensory illusion, of indoctrinated trance, to be clear about anything except at rare lucid intervals. In fact, trance states are much more prevalent than is generally realized; there really is no such thing as an "ordinary" state of consciousness.

"Man is asleep," said Ouspensky, and he really meant that we are all in a semiwaking, semisleeping trance induced by our whole cultural heritage and our personal belief system. To be fully awakened, we must be wholly aware of all the influences which bear upon our daily state of consciousness.

Perhaps in this regard, one of the most heartening trends today is the great interest people are taking in scientific discoveries relating to man's split brain. For many hundreds of years, the Sufis have said that man must learn to use his mind in a different way if he is to progress. That different way is the holistic, synthesizing, right-hemisphere way.

Too much attention should not be attached to the topographical implications in terms such as "right-hemisphere function." The various functions may or may not be neatly located in one or the other brain hemisphere (our guess is that they are *not*). The important thing is that there are unquestionably two types of brain functioning which may, for convenience, be termed "left-hemisphere-type function" and "right-hemisphere-type function," and this seems to have been known to Eastern students of meditation for several thousand years.

Our right hemisphere, with its capacity for appreciating a complex whole, for facial recognition, picture comprehension, map reading, maze solving, provides the alternative mode of understanding. It is not that there is anything wrong with the logical, time-sequential, step-by-step mode of thought, but that both modes are needed for a full understanding of and interaction with life.

Logic is fine for mentally running over the mistakes of the past and for planning the future so that we do not commit the same blunders twice. But life is here and now; we have to live in the present moment, in the present action. We are—all of us—at this very moment standing at the meeting point of two eternities: the immense past (which, as far as this earth is concerned, extends back six or seven thousand million years) and the unthinkable vastness of the future. We cannot actually live in either of these time realms, and the effort to do so may damage both our minds and our bodies.

Our task, then, is to learn to free ourselves from the cultural trance, the daydream of illusions, and, with an Awakened Mind, live life today.

The implications of our own research to date are clear. By applying modern electrophysiological measurement methods to the monitoring of Eastern techniques, it is possible to teach people methods of meditation best suited to their needs in a very short time.

By applying methods of measuring nervous-system response before and after meditation as we have shown in this book, or at intervals during training, it is possible to see not only how well pupils are learning to relax, but how much they have benefited, in a physical sense, from this relaxation.

From our aforementioned studies of the brain-wave patterns of some three thousand pupils, as well as swamis, yogis, Zen masters, healers, mediums and clairvoyants, it has become possible to establish that all the unusual abilities that some people are able to manifest (self-control of pain and healing, healing of others, telepathy, etc.) are associated with changes in the EEG pattern toward a more bilaterally symmetrical and integrated form.

Studies of individual patients referred by doctors for biofeedback training in relation to supposed neurological or neuromuscular disorders has shown that there is always some psychological difficulty, usually anxiety, and that the combined use of orthodox biofeedback and psychotherapy produces better results than either alone (sometimes orthodox biofeedback demands too much effort from a sick and confused patient).

People who enroll in classes just out of an interest in meditation and personal development often get greater benefits than those who seek to remedy some mental or physical disability and who work exclusively to that end.

Looking to the future, we see the need for a much broader range of specialized equipment than is at present available, and prototypes for some of these machines are now under construction—for instance, Mind Mirrors with a greater total frequency range, multiple-frequency stroboscopic lights to assist in the production of specific altered states of consciousness and electrical skin-resistance meters capable of showing much more profound levels of relaxation.

The possibilities inherent in the new Data Recorder must be explored to the full, for now that the heretofore invisible inner states of man, his body-mind interrelationships, can not only be made visible but can be recorded so that they can be repeated as statistical and scientific evidence for further study and practical use, there is no limit to where his development of higher states might lead.

But the work must also begin to move out of the laboratory into the classroom, clinic and consulting room. Already, to this end, we have been asked to assist several universities and clinics in setting up their own biofeedback or healing projects.

Our work with healers is taking many new directions, and there are so many possibilities for exploration that one could wish for forty-eight-hour days and month-long weeks, for of necessity, the work is slow, cannot be forced and requires, above all, infinite patience. Healers themselves are as anxious to learn and to apply our instrumented techniques as we are to experiment and to learn from them. And there is an unceasing call for lectures, information, and demonstration of our methods to a wide variety of professional, medical and scientific associations, as well as large conferences where the subject we have dealt with here is an increasing focus of attention.

All this makes it difficult to stop the book at this point, not to wait just a little longer, just until the next experiments, the next results. . . . But this is the story of any research that has broken new ground, and where the significance to mankind is inestimable.

Bibliography

Allison, J. "Respiratory Changes During the Practice of the Technique of Transcendental Meditation." *The Lancet*, no. 7651 (April, 1970), p. 883.

Anand, B. K., G. S. China, and B. Singh. "Some Aspects of EEG Studies in Yogis." *EEG and Clinical Neurophysiology* 13(1961): 432.

Anderson, M. L. "The Relations of Psi to Creativity." *Journal of Para-Psychology*, 26(1962):277.

Aquinas, T. *Summa Theologica*. New York: McGraw-Hill, 1964.

Aurobindo, Sri. *Essays of the Gita*. New York: Sri Aurobindo Library, 1950.

Austin, M. D. "Dream Recall and the Bias of Intellectual Ability." *Nature* 231(1971):59–68.

Baken, P. "Hypnotizability, Laterality of Eye Movements and Functional Brain Asymmetry." *Perceptual and Motor Skills* 28(1969):927.

Beaumont, J. G. "Handedness and Hemisphere Function." *In Hemisphere Function in the Human Brain*, edited by S. J. Diamond and J. G. Beaumont. New York: Halstead Press, 1974.

229

Benson, H. *The Relaxation Response.* New York: William Morrow & Co., 1975.

Blofeld, J. *The Tantric Mysticism of Tibet.* New York: E. P. Dutton, 1970.

Brazier, Mary A. B. *The Electrical Activity of the Nervous System.* Williams & Williams Co. Baltimore, 1968.

Broad, C. *Lectures on Psychical Research.* New York: Humanities Press, 1962.

Brown, Barbara B. "Awareness of EEG-Subjective Activity Relationships Detected with a Closed Feedback System." *Psychophysiology* 7(1970):451.

Brunton, P. *The Hidden Teaching Beyond Yoga.* New York: Samuel Weiser, 1972.

Bucke, R. M. *Cosmic Consciousness.* New York: E. P. Dutton, 1969.

Cade, C. Maxwell, and Woolley-Hart, Ann, M.D. M.S. B.S. "Psychophysiological Studies of Hypnotic Phenomena," *British Journal of Clinical Hypnosis* 5:(Jan–April 1974).

————. "Measurement of Hypnosis and Auto-Hypnosis by Determination of Electrical Skin Resistance." *Journal of Society for Psychical Research* 46:(June 1971).

Castaneda, C. *The Teaching of Don Juan: A Yaqui Way of Knowledge.* Berkeley: University of California Press, 1968.

Cocteau, J. "The Process of Inspiration." *The Creative Process,* edited by B. Ghiselin. Berkeley: University of California Press, 1952.

Conze, E. *Buddhist Meditation.* London: Allen & Unwin, 1955.

Coxhead, Nona. *Mindpower: The Emerging Pattern of Current Research.* London: Heinemann, 1976; Penguin, 1978. New York: St. Martin's Press, 1978.

Dasgupta, S. *Yoga as Philosophy and Religion.* London: Kegan Paul, 1924.

De Ropp, R. S. *The Master Game.* New York: Dell Publishing, 1968.

Dunbar, F. *Mind and Body: Psychosomatic Medicine.* New York: Random House, 1937.

Durchkeim, K. *Hara: The Vital Centre of Man*. London: Unwin, Mandala, 1977.

Evans-Wentz, W. Y. trans. *The Tibetan Book of the Dead*. New York: Oxford University Press, 1960.

———. *Tibetan Yoga*. New York: Oxford University Press, 1967.

Frankl, Victor E. *Man's Search for Meaning*. New York: Washington Square Press, 1970.

Fried, Edrita. *Artistic Productivity and Mental Health*. Springfield Ill.: C. C. Thomas, 1964.

Fromm, E., *et al*. *Zen Buddhism and Psychoanalysis*. London: Allen and Unwin, 1960.

Garrett, E. J. *Adventures in the Supernormal*. New York: Garrett Publications, 1949; New York: Paperback Library, 1968.

Gazzaniga, M. S. *The Bisected Brain*. New York: Appleton-Century-Crofts, 1970.

Goleman, D. "Meditation as Meta-Therapy: Hypotheses Toward a Proposed Fifth State of Consciousness." *Journal of Transpersonal Psychology* 3(1971):1–25.

Govinda, L. A. *Foundations of Tibetan Mysticism*. New York: E. P. Dutton, 1960.

Gowan, J. C. *The Development of the Creative Individual*. San Diego: Robert Knapp, 1972.

———. *Development of the Psychedelic Individual*. Buffalo: Creative Education Foundation, 1971.

Green, E. E., and Alyce Green. *Beyond Biofeedback*. London: Bell Press, 1978. New York, Delacorte Press, 1977.

Green, E. E., Alyce Green, and E. D. Walter, "Psychophysiological Training for Creativity." (mimeo), Topeka, Kan.: Menninger Clinic, Sept. 1971.

———. "Voluntary Control of Internal States." *Journal of Transpersonal Psychology* 2(1970): 1:1–26.

———. "Biofeedback for Mind-Body Self Regulation: Healing and Creativity." (mimeo), Topeka, Kan.: Menninger Clinic, 1971.

Happold, F. C. *The Journey Inwards*. London: Darton, Longman & Todd, Ltd., 1972.

Humphrey, M. E., and Zangwill, O. L. "Cessation of Dreaming

After Brain Injury." *Journal of Neurological Neurosurgical Psychiatry* 14(1951):125.

Humphreys, Christmas. *Concentration and Meditation.* Baltimore: Penguin Books (Pelican A1236), 1970.

————. *Zen: A Way of Life.* Boston: Little, Brown & Co., 1971.

————. *Zen Bhuddism.* New York: Macmillan, 1971.

Huxley, A. *The Perennial Philosophy.* New York: Harper Brothers, 1945.

Isaacson, R. L. *The Limbic System.* New York: Plenum Press, 1974.

James, W. *The Varieties of Religious Experience.* New York: Longman Green, 1902.

Jung, C. G. *Collected Works.* London: Routledge and Kegan Paul, 1977.

Kamiya, Joseph. "Conscious Control of Brain Waves." *Psychology Today* 1(April 1968):57.

Kieffer, Durham. "Meditation and Biofeedback." In *The Higher States of Consciousness,* edited by John White. New York: Doubleday, Anchor Books, 1972.

Koestler, A. *The Act of Creation.* New York: Macmillan, 1964.

Krippner, S. "Creativity and Psychic Phenomena." *Gifted Child Quarterly* 7(1963):51–56.

————. "The Creative Person and Non-Ordinary Reality." *Gifted Child Quarterly* 16(1972):203–228.

Lesh, T. V. "Zen Meditation and the Development of Empathy in Counsellors." and "Biofeedback and Self-control." *Aldine Annual,* 1970.

LeShan, L. *Toward a General Theory of the Paranormal.* New York: Parapsychological Foundation, 1969.

Levine, M. "Electrical Skin Resistance During Hypnosis." *Neurological Psychiatry* 24(1930):937–942.

Lilly, John C. *The Centre of the Cyclone.* New York: Julian Press, 1972.

Luria, A. R. *The Working Brain.* Trans. by B. Haigh. New York: Basic Books, 1973.

Luthe, W. "Autogenic Training: Method, Research, and Application in Medicine." In *Altered States of Consciousness*, edited by C. Tart. New York: John Wiley and Sons, 1969.

Mack, J. E. *Nightmares and Human Conflict*. Boston: Little, Brown & Co., 1970.

Maharishi Mahesh Yogi. *Commentary on the Bhagavad Gita*. Baltimore: Penguin Books, 1969.

Maslow, A. H. *Motivation and Personality*. New York: Harper Brothers, 1954.

————. *Toward a Psychology of Being*. Princeton: D. Van Nostrand, 1962.

————. *Religious Values and Peak Experiences*. Columbus: Ohio State University Press, 1964.

————. "The Creative Attitude." In *Explorations in Creativity*, edited by R. L. Mooney and T. A. Razik. New York: Harper & Row, 1967.

————. "A Theory of Metamotivation: The Biological Rooting of the Value-Life." *Journal of Humanistic Psychology* 7(1967):93–127.

————. *The Farther Reaches of Human Nature*. New York: Viking Press, 1971.

Masters, R. E. L. and Jean Houston. *The Varieties of Psychedelic Experience*. New York: Holt, Rinehart & Winston, 1966.

Maupin, E. W. "Responses to Zen Meditation Exercise." *Journal of Consulting Psychology* 23(1965):139.

McKellar, P. and L. Simpson. "Between Wakefulness and Sleep." *British Journal of Psychology* 45(1954):266.

Meares, Ainslie. *Relief Without Drugs*. London: Souvenir Press, 1968.

Naranjo, C., and R. E. Ornstein. *On the Psychology of Meditation*. New York: Viking Press, 1971.

Nyaponika, Thera. *The Heart of Buddhist Meditation*. London: Rider, 1962.

Ornstein, R. E. *The Psychology of Consciousness*. San Fransisco: W. H. Freeman & Co., 1973.

Ouspensky, P. D. *A New Model of the Universe*. London: Kegan Paul, 1938.

————. *In Search of the Miraculous*. New York: Harcourt Brace, 1949.

Patanjali, Bhagwan Shree. *Aphorisms of Yoga*. London: Faber & Faber, 1973.

Payne, B. *Getting There Without Drugs*. London: Wildwood House, 1973.

Pelletier, Kenneth. *Mind as Healer, Mind as Slayer*. New York: Delacorte Press/Seymour Lawrence, 1977.

Progoff, I., ed. *The Cloud of Unknowing*. New York: Julian Press, 1969.

Puharich, A. *Beyond Telepathy*. New York: Doubleday, 1962.

Rahula, Walpola. *What the Buddha Taught*. Surrey: Gordon Fraser Gallery Ltd., Bedford, 1959.

Richter, C. P. "Sleep Produced by Hypnotics Studied by the Electrical Skin Resistance Method." *Journal of the Pharmacological Experimental Therapy* 42(1931):471–485.

Roberts, J. *The Seth Material*. Englewood Cliffs, N.J.: Prentice Hall, 1970.

————. *Seth Speaks*. Englewood Cliffs, N.J.: Prentice Hall, 1972.

Rogers, C. R. *Client Centered Therapy*. Boston: Houghton Miflin. 1951.

————. *On Becoming a Person*. Boston: Houghton Miflin. 1961.

Roll, W. G. "Psychic Research in Relation to Higher States of Consciousness." In *The Highest State of Consciousness*, edited by T. White, pp. 456–471. New York: Anchor Books, 1972.

Rossi, E. L. *Dreams and the Growth of Personality*. New York: Pergamon Press, 1972.

————. "The Cerebral Hemispheres in Analytical Psychology." *Journal of Analytical Psychology*, Jan. 1977.

Saraswati, Swami Prakashanad. *The Science of Devotion and Grace*. Brindabar, India: International Society of Divine Love, 1975.

Schmeidler, G. and L. Lewis. "Mood Changes after Alpha Feedback Training." *Perceptual and Motor Skills*, no. 32 (June 1971), pp. 709–710.

Schultz, J. and W. Luthe. *Autogenic Training: A Psychophysiological Approach in Psychotherapy*. New York: Grune & Stratton, 1959.

Shah, I. *Tales of the Dervishes*. London: Jonathan Cape, 1967.

————. *The Magic Monastery*. London: Jonathan Cape, 1972.

Stace, W. T. *The Teaching of the Mystics*. New York: Mentor, 1960.

Stanford, R. G. and C. R. Lovin. "The EEG Alpha Rhythm and ESP Performances." *Journal of the American Society for Psychical Research* 64(1970):4.

Stevenson, I. *Telepathic Impressions*. Charlottesville: The University of Virginia Press, 1970.

Stoyva, J. and J. Kamiya. "Electrophysiological Studies of Dreaming and the Prototype of a New Strategy in the Study of Consciousness." *Psychological Review* 75(May, 1968):192–205.

Sudhu Monni. *Meditation*. Hollywood: Wilshire Books, 1967.

Sullivan, H. S. The *Interpersonal Theory of Psychiatry*. New York: W. W. Norton, 1953.

Suzuki, D. T. *An Introduction to Zen Buddhism*. New York: Grove Press, 1964.

Tart, C. T. *On Being Stoned*. Science and Behaviour Books, 1971.

Tart, C. T. ed. *Altered States of Consciousness*. New York: Wiley & Sons, 1969.

————. *Transpersonal Psychologies*. New York: Harper & Row, 1975.

Troward, T. *The Edinburgh Lectures on Mental Science*. New York: Robert McBridie, 1909.

Tyrrell, G. W. N. *Apparitions*. New York: Society for Psychical Research, 1953.

Ullman, M. Krippner, S. and Vaughan, A. *Dream Telepathy*. New York: Macmillan, 1973.

Walker, K. *Diagnosis and Man*. (A332 Pelican) Penguin Books, 1962.

————. A *Study of Gurdjieff's Teaching*. London: Jonathan Cape, 1957.

Wallace, R. K. "Physiological Effects of Transcendental Meditation: A Proposed Fourth Major State of Consciousness." *Science* 166(March 1969):1751–1754.

Wallace, R. K. and H. Benson. "The Physiology of Meditation."
    Scientific American 226(Feb. 1972)2:89.
Wallace, R. K., Benson, H. and A. F. Wilson. "A Wakeful Hypo-
    metabolic State." *American Journal of Physiology* 221(1971):3,
    795.
Watson, L. *Supernature.* New York: Doubleday, 1973.
Weil, Andrew. *The Natural Mind.* Boston: Houghton Miflin,
    1972.
White, J. ed. *The Highest State of Consciousness.* New York:
    Doubleday, 1972.
Yogananda, P. *Autobiography of a Yogi.* Los Angeles: SRF Pub-
    lishers, 1946.
Young, J. Z. "Why Do We Have Two Brains?" In *Inter-*
    hemispheric Relations and Cerebral Dominance, edited by
    V. B. Mentcastle. Baltimore: The Johns Hopkins University Press,
    1962.

Appendix A

Mind Mirror Patterns and Diagrams

Represented here are sixteen new patterns of state five on the Mind Mirror, which have been confirmed since the book was completed. They are added to show the already expanding realm of potentially confirmable states of consciousness and the possibilities that lie ahead in the work of measurable physiological correlates of inner states.

The diagrams represent the display panel of the Mind Mirror. No activity at all would be represented by two parallel lines down the center of the panel. Movement of the pattern away from the center to the left indicates activity from the left hemisphere of the brain, and from the center to the right represents activity of the right hemisphere. As discussed previously, the left hemisphere is assumed to be dominant and responsible for logical thinking, while the right deals with the whole pattern, the gestalt and logical thinking. (These categories are likely to be true for two subjects out of three only, and this should be kept in mind during the following explanations of the Mind Mirror patterns.) The sensitivity of the instrument will normally be set at 10 microvolts.

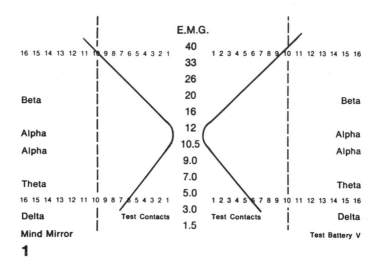

Diagram 1. *We call this response passive awareness or alpha blocking. Note the high amplitude of the delta frequencies, which traditionally have only been associated with deep sleep. Presumably, in the many experiments concerning alpha states and alpha blocking, the delta was not expected and therefore was not seen, though the beta frequencies were noted because they fitted the model: that beta is associated with mental activity. The filters which separated the alpha frequencies would, of course, reject both the beta and the delta, and so if delta was seen, it was probably assumed to have been an artifact. Others, though, have reported the delta response in the waking state, notably Luria, who in* The Working Brain, *gives many spectral diagrams of waking responses, all showing delta. Our suggestion is that delta is to be interpreted as a reaching out to the not yet known in a passive way.*

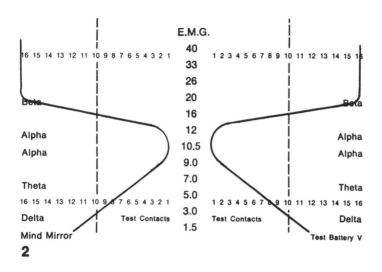

E.M.G.

Mind Mirror

2

Test Battery V

Diagram 2 *also represents passive awareness, but perhaps a little less so. It is the usual response from a subject who is having a first encounter with the Mind Mirror. The novelty of seeing one's brain rhythms soon wears off and the pattern reverts to that shown in Diagram 1. Therefore, wait a few moments rather than adjusting the sensitivity of the Mind Mirror. The diagrams so far show symmetrical responses, as they will be if the subject is an average meditator. Alternatively, they could be measured from a subject who would deny ever having had any experience of meditation but who is reasonably relaxed and who does not allow a new situation to perturb his stillness.*

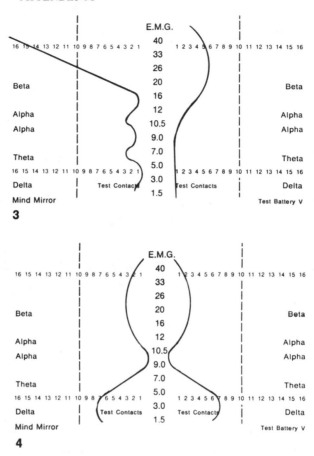

Diagram 3 *is the pattern of a not very still person. The left shows only beta activity, the alarm reaction of the sympathetic nervous system, which inhibits the activity of the right hemisphere.*

Diagram 4 *shows a very calm person. Beta represents the alarm aspect of mental activity, while complex thought need not be accompanied by any beta activity whatsoever. A calm person may be very alert, directing his mental content as he wishes, and yet show only a small response in the beta range.*

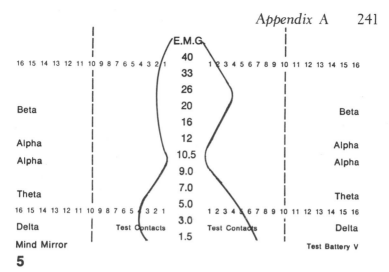

5

Diagram 5 *represents a similar pattern to Diagram 4. There is no trace of an alarm reaction from the left hemisphere, but the significance of the right beta seems to be that the subject is intuiting the meaning of his experience. The right beta reaction may also be seen during dream recall and therefore is a confirmation that the right is indeed the holistic hemisphere.*

As an aside to the discussion of these patterns, it must be said that it is not easy to determine which hemisphere is the dominant one. Obviously, in Diagram 3, the left is clearly dominant, since it is the only one which is being allowed to function. Sometimes asking the subject to perform complex mental arithmetic (such as to subtract 9 times 9 from 11 times 11 and multiply the answer by 3) will indicate the dominant hemisphere by an alarm reaction to the test situation, but many subjects can perform such calculations and remain calm. The following example is given to show how easy it is to allow one's preconceptions to cause errors: A subject performing complex arithmetic showed right beta activity. However, intuition suggested that he was left dominant, and so he was asked to explain how the calculation had been performed. His reply showed that he had visualized a blackboard with the numbers on it and then allowed the problem to solve itself—a twin-hemisphere method of performing arithmetic!

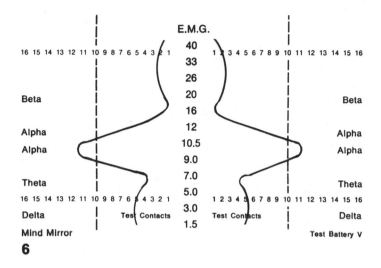

E.M.G.

Mind Mirror

6

Test Battery V

Diagram 6 *is the pattern of a meditator with his eyes shut. Note the symmetry of the patterns, which becomes permanent once the initial difficulties, if any, of beginning meditation are overcome. The dominant frequency of the alpha peak becomes lower during meditation and is also a very approximate indication of how long meditation (or stillness) has been practiced.*

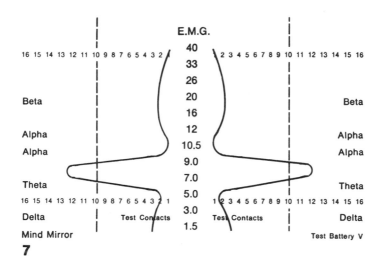

E.M.G.

16 15 14 13 12 11 10 9 8 7 6 5 4 3 2 1   40   2 3 4 5 6 7 8 9 10 11 12 13 14 15 16
                                          33
                                          26
Beta   20   Beta
                                          16
Alpha   12   Alpha
Alpha   10.5   Alpha
                                          9.0
                                          7.0
Theta   5.0   Theta
16 15 14 13 12 11 10 9 8 7 6 5 4 3 2 1   3.0   1 2 3 4 5 6 7 8 9 10 11 12 13 14 15 16
Delta   Test Contacts   1.5   Test Contacts   Delta
Mind Mirror   Test Battery V

7

Diagram 7. *We find that at the first introduction to meditation, the initial pattern will be peaked at 12 Hertz or higher, while two to five years' experience causes the alpha frequency to reduce to 9 Hertz and with from ten to twenty years' practice, we find the alpha frequency around 7 Hertz, as represented in Diagram 7. After meditation, these patterns will remain for a while as the subject resumes his usual routine; he holds that state which Maharishi has called the afterglow of meditation; that state which Goleman used to call state five, when the separation between the meditative experience and the rest of one's life now begins to diminish; this state is the first step toward the Awakened Mind.*

We find that all healers show the state-five pattern, though it may only appear when they are healing, and we have noted that they induce the same pattern in their patients, even though the patients could never produce such a pattern at any other time.

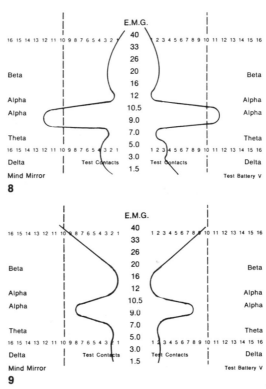

8

9

Diagram 8. *In the description of passive awareness, it was suggested that delta frequencies in the waking state represented a reaching out to the not yet known; such frequencies are often found added to the healer's state-five pattern, particularly when he is altering his intention toward the patient or trying to match the needs of the patient. That delta may be connected with the paranormal is supported by a paper, "Ramp functions in EEG power spectra during actual or attempted paranormal events," by Dr. Joel L. Whitton of Toronto.*

Diagram 9. *Healers are human and so will sometimes show an alarm reaction added to the state-five pattern during the unusual situation of being connected to a machine while healing. This beta reaction will usually vanish after a while.*

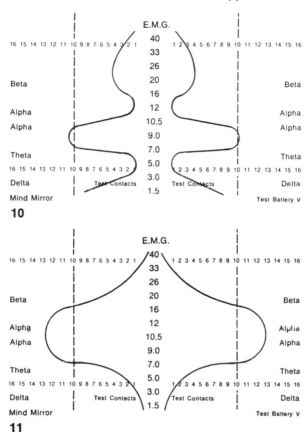

Diagram 10. *Symmetrical delta has been found with many subjects and notably with one boy who is reputed to bend metal mentally; he shows delta peaks of fifteen microvolts.*

Diagram 11. *Active creativity, state six. We believe this to be the state beyond the Awakened Mind. The power spectrum is even across the whole of the alpha band; we have measured this with a few rare individuals, notably the Swami Prakashanand Saraswati (see Chapter 7). This state seems to be a total creative response to a situation but is never maintained for very long.*

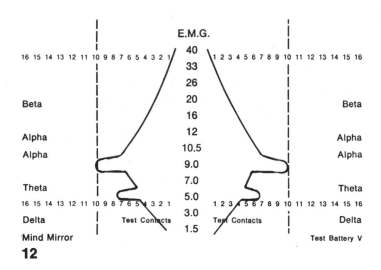

Diagram 12. *All these rather precise levels so far described should be considered as signposts on a continuous path, one level flowing into the next as progress is made and confirmed. The journey, too, is not to be thought of as slow, steady progress but rather should be seen as fleeting, transitory jumps to higher levels, less and less time being spent at the lower ones until the transition becomes permanent. Diagram 12 shows a combination of states five and six, Diagrams 6 and 11; among others, Maxwell Cade has shown this pattern.*

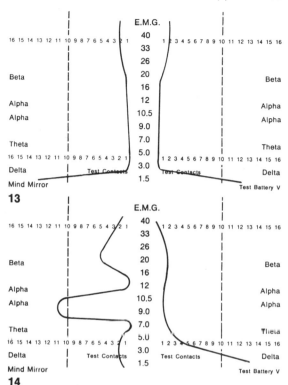

Diagram 13. *Referring to the table of Lesh states (pages 24–25), it will be seen that at extremely deep levels of physical relaxation, both alpha and theta have disappeared and only delta remains. This is not a sleep state, however; the difference of palmar skin resistance shows this, being around 80 percent change, whereas in nondreaming sleep, the skin resistance change would be no more than 50 percent.*

Diagram 14. *We believe that this pattern graphically demonstrates what is meant by Jung's transcendent function—the ability to use the two halves of the cortex appropriately and independently. A healer we tested often shows this pattern when with a patient but reverts to state five when he is "charging his batteries."*

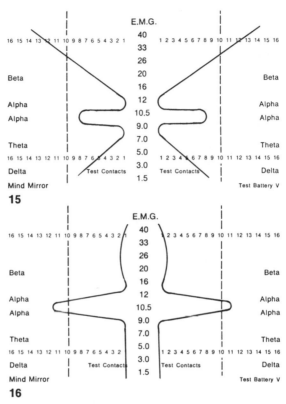

Diagram 15 *represents passive awareness, but the alpha peak should be noted; the subject is performing in a parapsychological experment. A possible explanation is that there is a below-threshold stimulus, the ESP event, and the alpha peak exists because the reticular activating system is increasing the cortical awareness in an attempt to bring the stimulus into consciousness.*

Diagram 16. *Nothing but alpha, the pattern of level 2, the hypnagogic and hypnapompic state characterized by rapid, changeable, dreamlike images. Sometimes a subject may slip toward sleep into the state instead of meditation, in which case only alpha will be present.*

Appendix B

Technical Descriptions of the Machines

The *Omega 1 Electrical Skin Resistance Meter* has three components: a microammeter, a low-impedance voltage-setting circuit and a stabilized voltage so that exact values of basal resistance, measured in ohms, may be determined.

The change of electrical skin resistance is indicated by levels of voltage and current, which have been chosen to give a reasonably accurate indication over the range required. Errors are caused at one limit by voltages generated at the surface of the skin due to acidity of perspiration and at the other limit by high voltages causing depolarization of the sweat membrane. Due to these two constraints, we do not use constant-current methods of measurement.

The *Monitor-M* combines the functions of an electroencephalograph and an electromyograph to indicate electrical brain rhythms and muscular tensions respectively. Switching allows either left or right hemisphere to be measured or, alternatively, two muscle positions. In the EEG mode, the filters have an excellent flat-top response in the alpha, beta, theta and delta ranges, with rejections of 36 decibels per octave at the edges of each band. The meter may also show the exact frequency of the dominant brain rhythm being produced.

There are four settings of sensitivity at 3, 10, 30 and 100 microvolts for full-scale meter reading. Carefully chosen input transistors give noise levels below 0.2 microvolts in any one channel. Differential input considerably reduces the effects of external interference, such as that received from house wiring. The input is also protected from radio interference from sources such as short-wave or citizen-band radio. There is an indication of artifact levels when the signal contains a component in the band 100–200 Hertz, which is above 100 microvolts in level. Input overload does not occur until the input level exceeds 73 decibels. There is an optocoupled output from the integrated signal.

The *Temperature Meter* with *Thermistor Probe* indicates changes of half a degree Centigrade up and down. When the needle is set to the center of the meter scale, the balance control indicates the temperature. The detector is the small thermistor which is taped to the hand.

We find that this meter forms a very good introduction to biofeedback because beginners are surprised to find how much control they have over their blood flow by means of visualization.

The Mind Mirror is an electroencephalograph which was specially designed to show in a positive, immediate way the brain rhythms of both hemispheres of the cortex simultaneously. The display consists of twenty-four rows of light-emitting diodes (LEDs) set sixteen to the row, with the display response limited as far as possible only by the filters so that ephemeral patterns are seen, whereas most EEGs are not designed for such display.

The original requirement was formulated by C. Maxwell Cade in 1974, and the first prototype was used in one of his courses on June 1, 1976.

The EEG uses electrodes attached to the head to pick up the voltages generated by the brain. These voltages are very severely attenuated as they pass through bone and tissue so that only millionths of a volt are available. The input pream- plifier must, therefore, be very sensitive and is also balanced to eliminate as far as possible unwanted potentials from elec- tric light supplies. After some amplification, the signals pass to an electronic attenuator to keep them at a suitable level for the display. After the attenuator, the signal is separated into two paths, one having a pass band of 1 Hertz to 45 Hertz for the twelve left-hand channels, while the other passes signals between 100 and 300 Hertz, serving the myograph channel shown in the thirteenth row of green LEDs. This is similarly repeated for the right-hand channels.

Each channel consists of a four-pole filter, which gives a flat response over the desired band with an excellent rejection of other frequencies. The signal from the filter is applied to a complex, integrated circuit, which converts the integrated analogue signal into a position on a row of light-emitting diodes.

The apparatus is voltage calibrated, making it possible to measure accurately the strength of the signal in each one of the frequency channels. Muscle activity in the scalp or neck may generate voltages which interfere with the brain-rhythm measurement, so the Mind Mirror has a channel for each side of the head, showing in lights of a different color the strength of any such unwanted signal. Relaxation exercises will usually reduce these tensions to a low level. The myo- graph channel may therefore be used to obtain extra data regarding the subject's anxiety.

There is also a means to switch the first four rows of diodes into a resistance check of the effectiveness of the contact at the scalp. A second test switches one row into a voltage check to measure the battery state. A third switch enables an oscillator to operate so that all channels may be checked for sensitivity.

Further controls allow some of the channels to control a tone for normal feedback purposes. This may be connected in a number of different ways according to the subject's (or customer's) requirements. One possibility allows up to three channels to be added together by top-panel switches for feedback. A separate option allows one of the twenty-four-way sockets to be used as a patch connector so that any combination of three channels may be used to control the tone-feedback oscillator.

An alternative use for this output socket allows all the filter voltages to be examined before integration. The second socket offers the unfiltered outputs from the two channels for recording purposes, plus attenuator-level indication. A further two connections allow a recorded signal to be fed back into the Mind Mirror for reviewing.

The Data Recorder. We required a facility which would record two Mind Mirrors simultaneously, together with other data such as elapsed time, electrical skin resistance and EMG signals. Data from conventional paper recorders is far too bulky, and not everyone has access to the floppy disc recorders of the normal computer system.

We therefore decided to use the standard small magnetic tape cassette. Pulse-position modulation was chosen at a basic frequency of 1024 Hertz, with eight channels, each having a response of DC to 50 Hertz with a signal-to-noise ratio of 40 decibels.

The pulse-position modulation carries the analog signal directly or a digitally coded signal when an eight-bit code is employed. Such data as elapsed time and reference numbers do not require fast updating, so all these arc compressed into one of the channels which is arranged as eight words of eight bits, the whole frame being synchronized every half-second.

If all four tracks are used on the cassette, then other information may be recorded, or voice may be added to one track. A variant of this system allows us to transmit the data by radio, and without decoding the signal at the receiver, we can insert further information, such as time before recording, onto the cassette.

Appendix C

Biofeedback Instrument Manufacturers

The Mind Mirror EEG, the Omega 1 ESR meter, the cassette data recorder and relaxation tapes are available from:

In England—Audio Ltd.
      26 Wendell Road
      London W12 9RT

In the USA—Coherent Communications
      13733 Glenoaks Boulevard
      Sylmar, Calif. 91342

In Canada—Roth Corporation
      P.O. Box 333
      Willowdale, Ont. M2N 5S9

Audio Ltd. also has a less complex EEG which has an EMG (electromyograph) facility and a temperature meter. Such instruments are also available in the USA from:

Aquarius Electronics, P.O. Box 96, Albion, Calif. 95410

Autogenic Systems, Inc., 809 Allston Way, Berkeley, Calif. 94710

Biofeedback Instruments, 126 Harvard Street, Brookline, Mass. 02146

Biofeedback Research Institute, Inc., 6325 Wilshire Blvd. Los Angeles, Calif. 90048

Bioscan Corporation, P.O. Box 14168, Houston, Tex. 77021

Colbourn Instruments, Inc., Box 2551, Lehigh Valley, Pa. 18001

Cyborg Corporation, 342 Western Ave., Boston, Mass. 02135

Huma Tech Industries, 1725 Rogers Ave., San Jose, Calif. 95112

J & J Enterprises, 22797 Holgar Ct., N.E. Poulsbo, Wash. 98370

Schneider Instrument Co., 9631 Gross Point Road, Skokie, Ill. 60076

In Australia—Mind Force Australia
P.O. Box 771
Parramatta 2150 NSW

Appendix D

Glossary of Technical Terms

Abreaction. A process of releasing a repressed emotion by reliving in imagination the original experience.

Affective. Any kind of feeling attached to ideas or idea complexes belonging to the *left hemisphere*, which, when it reaches a certain physiological level, causes changes in the blood chemistry.

Alpha. The range of electrical activity of the brain which is changing between 8 and 13 times per second.

Altered State of Consciousness. A state in which the individual clearly feels a qualitative shift in his pattern of mental functioning; see *Peak experience, Self-remembering*.

Amygdala. The small structure resting at the ends of the *hippocampus* in the *limbic system* (the "emotional" brain). Stimulation can produce anything from blind rage to euphoria.

Arousal. The state of activity of the *sympathetic nervous system*, also called the *fight-or-flight response*, which can be given an accurate quantitive measurement defined by the apparent electrical resistance of the skin.

Artifact. An unwanted signal which could lead to error in interpretation of an instrument indication.

Autonomic nervous system (ANS). Consisting of the *sympathetic* and the *parasympathetic* nervous systems, this system deals with everyday bodily functions such as maintenance of heartbeat, blood pressure, regular breathing and digestion of food. Formerly thought to be involuntary, but now known to be susceptible to conscious control.

Back EMF (Electro Motive Force) of polarization. The electrical voltage barrier generated at the sweat-gland membrane.

Basal skin resistance (BSR). The characteristic value of an individual's apparent electrical skin resistance.

Beta. The electrical activity of the brain which changes within the range of 13 to 25 times per second.

Bilateral. A term referring to both the left and the right hemispheres of the brain.

Biofeedback. The process whereby, through the use of some technical device, one can become aware of an internal event of which one is not normally aware, in order to learn to control some aspect of that event.

Brain stem. A thick, trunklike structure ascending from the spinal cord containing the *reticular activating system,* the center for arousing and alerting the *cortex.*

Central nervous system. The voluntary nervous system, which includes the brain and the nerves that direct skeletal muscle activity; it is concerned with thought, voluntary action and manipulation of the external environment through the limbs.

Cognitive. The linear, rational mode of knowledge of the *left hemisphere.*

Collective preconscious. The synonym for collective or group unconscious mind, the repository of archetypes.

Conceptualizing. The forming of a concept by the *left hemisphere* of the brain.

Consciousness. The totality of the contents of an individual's mind, both external and internal, involving his whole relation to his world.

Correlate. The term applied to the tendency of two series of measurements to vary concomitantly, in consequence of which knowledge of one gives a basis for drawing conclusions about the other.

Cortex, cerebral cortex. The part of the brain that is divided into two hemispheres, *left* and *right*, with opposite modes of functioning, which are joined by a large bundle of interconnecting fibers called the corpus callosum; it is dependent for arousal on the *reticular activating system.*

Dantien. Chinese term for Saiketanden.

Deep psychophysiological relaxation (DPR). A restful *hypometabolic* state, due to decreased activity of the *sympathetic nervous system;* mental and bodily stillness, leading to relief of stress symptoms and all kinds of physical benefits. See *relaxation response.*

Delta. The electrical activity of the brain changing within the range of ½ to 4 times per second; primarily associated with deep sleep.

Dissociation. A state in which the locus of a particular function shifts in the body more than it does in the brain, and vice versa, thereby rendering brain and body out of alignment.

Dysplasia. A type of body build not conforming to any of Kretschmer's three types of "athletic," "asthenic" and "pyknic." The "athletic" type seems biologically a milder form of the African Negro physique. The "asthenic" type historically seems to spring from chimpanzees and the earlier Aryan races. The "pyknic" type in many ways seems to hark back to the Mongol races and the orangutang.

Efferent impulses. Use of nerve fibers conducting impulses from the nervous center outward to muscle or gland.

Eidetic. A type of vivid imagery which is projected into the external world and is not merely in one's head.

Electrometric. A term meaning "electrically measured."

Electrical skin resistance (ESR). "Skin resistance" is a misleading, though long-established, term. What is actually measured in biofeedback arousal meters is a "Back EMF" of polarization, which in turn depends on local bloodflow. Sweat-gland activity is only a minor, secondary effect. Ultimately, what is being measured is arousal, that is, the *fight-or-flight response* or the *relaxation or trophotropic response.*

Electroencephalograph (EEG). A biofeedback instrument which monitors brain rhythms, usually by a tone feedback.

Electromyograph (EMG). A biofeedback device used in muscular-relaxation training to measure the degree of muscular tension as a consequence of stress.

Empathy. The ability to feel the emotions of others as if they were your own.

Enlightenment. The highest state of consciousness—cosmic or objective consciousness—in which there is a union between the individual's consciousness and the group unconscious with full cognitive control, one which permanently transforms the individual. (The term is used differently by Erich Fromm to denote *fifth-state consciousness.*)

Fifth-state consciousness. A way of being in which the stillness of the meditative state is sustained beyond the act of meditation and infuses the active waking consciousness, which allows the individual to carry out his everyday activities with full awareness. In this case, the alpha and theta reactions, generally associated with meditation, are present with the beta reactions of ordinary wakefulness. This way of being may pass (*sabikalpa samadhi*), but if it persists, the individual continues to complete *nirbikalpa samadhi.*

Fight-or-flight response. Reaction to inner or outer stress which literally prepares the individual for fighting or running away by increasing blood pressure, heart rate, breathing rate, body metabolism or rate of burning fuel and the flow of blood to the muscles of the arms and legs. See *Sympathetic nervous system.*

Frontalis muscle. The forehead muscle which usually contracts when a person is tense and overaroused. Its movement can be detected and fed back to the person through an *electromyograph* machine.

Gain setting. Adjustment of an instrument to give the desired sensitivity of response.

Galvanic skin response (GSR). A response which indicates the subject's state of arousal (*fight-or-flight* response) through fluctuations in the amount of sweat in the palm or fingertips, thereby affecting the *electrical skin resistance*.

Gestalt. An entire situation viewed from the emotional as well as the cognitive mode. Also a system of psychology which insists on seeing the individual as a whole. Therapy consists of returning the person to present-centeredness and the non- and preverbal realities of his inner and outer experience through a dramatic enactment of hidden conflicts in dreams, body gestures, and so on.

Hara. Seat of the vital powers. See *Saiketanden, Dantien*

Hertz (Hz.). The symbol for the number of electrical changes per second, used in measurement of brain rhythms.

Hippocampus. The largest structure of the *limbic system* (the "emotional" brain), essential to learning. Processes data from short-term to long-term memory.

Hyperesthesia. Increased sensitivity to tactual stimuli.

Hypermetabolic. Aroused physiological state brought about by increased *sympathetic nervous system* activity invoked by the *fight-or-flight* response.

Hypnoidal state. A state resembling sleep; used of conditions having some of the characteristics of the borders of sleep or light hypnosis.

Hypnogogostat. A biofeedback instrument designed to hold the state between waking and sleeping. The subject presses a button and, as he relaxes into the hypnogogic state, muscular tension disappears. He then releases the button, which causes a buzzer to sound, so making the subject aware of the threshold between the two states.

Hypnogogic. Transition from waking to sleeping, accompanied by vivid imagery.

Hypnopsychedelic. An experiential investigation of the factors which affect the production of parapsychological phenomena in *altered states of consciousness*.

Hypnopompic. Transition from sleeping to waking accompanied by vivid imagery.

Hypnosis. A state of deep relaxation which the patient induces in himself under the guidance of a therapist. See *Self-hypnosis*.

Hypometabolic. A restful state brought about by decreased activity of the *sympathetic nervous system*. See *Parasympathetic, Trophotropic* or *Relaxation response*.

Hypothalamus. Regulates certain vital functions such as fat and carbohydrate metabolism, temperature, hunger, thirst, sleep. Contains the central mechanism involving autonomic control; involved in both the *fight-or-flight* response and the *relaxation response*.

Ideoplasty. Literally, the physiological realization of an idea; points practically to the possibility of implanting an idea in the *right hemisphere*, which will work continually to manifest itself in external reality, in order to bring about unconsciously the desired physiological and psychological change.

Interoception. Reaction to stimuli from within the body, both from muscles, tendons and ligaments (*proprioception*), and from organs such as the heart, lungs, intestines, bladder. Can be conscious (as in *passive volition*) or unconscious.

Kilohms. A measurement in thousands of ohms, the unit of electrical resistance.

Left hemisphere. That part of the *cerebral cortex* which is predominantly involved with linear, time-sequential, analytic, linguistic, logical thinking; see *cognitive*. (It should be remembered that all statements in this book which contain the terms "left hemisphere" and "right hemisphere" refer not to specific areas of the cerebral cortex but to particular types of mental functioning. The reason for this, as explained in Chapter One, is that left-hemisphere-type thinking occasionally takes place in the right hemisphere, and vice versa. However, for about two-thirds of the population this distinction is unnecessary.)

Limbic. The primitive mammalian emotional brain lying between and linking the *cerebral cortex* and the *brain stem*.

Lesh. Dr. Terry Lesh is the originator of a scale of readings, the Lesh scale, which provides a correlation between specific subjective states of feeling and objective measurable physiological changes.

Meditation. A state of *deep physiological relaxation*, accompanied by alpha and theta brain rhythms. Though frequently initiated by a deliberate restriction of attention to a single or repeated stimulus, it leads eventually to a state of heightened and more inclusive awareness. When meditation becomes not simply an act but a way of being which infuses and transforms the ordinary waking consciousness, the individual has reached *fifth-state consciousness.*

Megohm. A measurement in millions of ohms, the unit of electrical resistance.

Mental fluency. The ability to manipulate one's mental contents freely.

Meta-syntactic. Gowan's term for the highest mode of knowing, in which the person has a full intuitive grasp of the entire situation.

Microampere. Millionth of an ampere, the unit of electrical current. Voltage resistance and current are related to each other by $V = IR$.

Mindfulness. The art of giving one's whole attention to the changing content of one's awareness (or a particular part of one's total awareness) without choosing the contents and without clinging to a particular content once another intrudes upon it. Traditionally, the technique of the Buddha.

Neural behavior. The behavior of the neurons or nerve impulses, the structural units of the nervous system.

Neural response. The response of a *neuron* or nerve impulse.

Neuron. The structural unit of the nervous system, or nerve impulse, consisting of a cell body with its processes.

Neurophysical type. A classification of physical types in terms of their physiology.

Neurophysiology. Branch of physiology which deals with the functional aspect of the nervous system, in particular, the investigation of the nature and transmission of the nerve impulse, or *neuron.*

Nirbikalpa samadhi. A term used by Yogananda (in *Autobiography of a Yogi*) to describe a higher state achieved by continuous meditation (*fifth-state consciousness*) in which an individual can move freely in the world and perform his outward duties without any loss of his "oneness of Spirit." See *Sabikalpa samadhi.*

Noetic. The intellectual mode of knowing of the *left hemisphere,* as contrasted with the intuitive mode of knowing of the *right hemisphere.*

Ohms. The unit of electrical resistance to the flow of electrical current.

Operant conditioning. A term used originally by B. F. Skinner to denote voluntary learning susceptible to reinforcements of reward or punishment.

Parasympathetic. A part of the *autonomic nervous system* that is the opposite of the *sympathetic nervous system.* It is invoked by the *relaxation response,* which counteracts the effects of stress.

Parameter. A unit which can be used in learning or growth curves, which differs with conditions, subjects, materials and so on.

Parataxic. Gowan's term for a mode of knowing through archetype, myth, ritual, drama, art. See *Right hemisphere.*

Passive volition. A conscious awareness of outgoing impulses in the autonomic nervous system. See *Voluntary control of internal states.*

Peak experience. A term coined by Maslow to describe a "moment in the life of the individual when he feels strong, sure, and in complete control." See *Self-actualization.*

Physiological. Belonging to that branch of biological science called physiology; concerned with the functioning of the structure and organs in a living organism.

Preconscious. An intermediate region between consciousness and the unconscious, where the material is at the moment unconscious but is available and ready to become conscious.

Proprioception. The reaction to internal stimuli from muscles, tendons, ligaments and so on. Can be conscious or unconscious. See *Interoception.*

Prosopopesis. Term coined by Durand LeGros to denote any sudden change in the personality, whether spontaneous or induced.

Prototaxic. Gowan's term for the most primitive way of knowing, when knowledge is registered in the body, as for example, in a blush.

Psychedelia. Term used by Gowan to describe an *altered state of consciousness* characterized by a sudden, spasmodic, transitory illumination in which the individual's consciousness is informed by the contents of the group unconscious with full cognitive control, but the transformation is not lasting.

Psychocybernetics. Practical, empirical branch of psychology which employs mechanistic techniques to increase the individual's self-awareness and well-being.

Psychophysiological. Pertaining to both psychological and physiological factors. The psychophysiological principle claims that any inner mental state has an objectively measurable physiological effect, and vice versa; See *Idioplasty*.

Psychosynthesis. A term used by Roberto Assagioli to refer to the reconstruction of the personality around a new center, a union of the personal with the transpersonal self.

Psychotechnics. A practical, humanistic branch of psychology which teaches those skills requisite to self-awareness, self-understanding and self-control. The aim is to enable the individual to become what he already is in potentiality; see *Self-actualization*.

Rapid eye movement (REM) sleep. The kind of sleep in which dreaming takes place, indicated by rapid movements of the closed eyes. REM sleep alternates with nonrapid eye movement sleep (NREM) throughout the night, and is essential to mental and physical well-being.

Relaxation response. Defined by Herbert Benson as being the response which is the reverse of the *fight-or-flight response*. It counteracts the effects of increased *sympathetic nervous system activity* and is, therefore, highly beneficial to the organism. See *Parasympathetic nervous system*.

Resistance. A reaction to the passage of electrical current, measured in ohms.

Reticular activating system (RAS). A tiny but very important nerve network in the central part of the *brain stem*, which has a critical role in determining states of awareness and levels of arousal.

Reynaud's disease. A condition of poor circulation due to muscular tension, which leaves the extremities of the body very cold. Relief of stress restores the circulation (see *Relaxation response*).

Reverie. A state of deep relaxation associated with hypnagogiclike imagery in which unconscious mental processes are revealed to the waking self as symbols, words or complex patterns.

Right hemisphere. That part of the *cerebral cortex* which is predominantly involved with holistic, simultaneous, relational ways of perceiving and knowing. It also holds the self-concept and the body image. See *Idioplasty, Left hemisphere.*

Rinzai Zen. A way of Zen which emphasizes the attempted solving of insoluble *koans* (paradoxes to be meditated upon) to totally frustrate the rational categories of the ego so that they are transcended.

Sabikalpa Samadhi. Term used by Yogananda to describe the *altered state of consciousness* where the devotee attains temporary realization of his oneness with spirit but cannot maintain it except in the immobile trance state. It is the state before *fifth-state consciousness.* See *Nirbikalpa samadhi.*

Saiketanden. Japanese term for the Hara center: two-finger breadth below the navel, seat of vital powers.

Samadhi. The continuous experience of *satori.*

Satori. Instantaneous, transient, partial enlightenment.

Seedless meditation. A state with no mental content, just awareness of being aware.

Selective inattention. The term used by Ouspensky to describe the process whereby anything which has been labeled unimportant is subsequently unperceived.

Self-actualization. Defined by Maslow as the act or process of manifesting the capabilities for which one has the potentiality.

Self-hypnosis. An *altered state of consciousness* accompanied by increased suggestibility.

Self-remembering. Gurdjieff's description for a state of heightened consciousness in which the individual is intensely aware of himself as well as the contents of his experience, whether inner or outer. See *Altered state of consciousness.*

Sensory deprivation. The nearly total reduction of input from the senses, resulting both in a state of acute mental confusion, which progresses to hallucination, and in a spontaneous healing of stress-related diseases such as colds and rashes.

Somnambulism. The practice of walking or other complex activities during sleep.

Soto Zen. A way of Zen which emphasizes a detached watching of the stream of consciousness, including the practice of just sitting.

Subvocalization. The silent miming of sounds in the throat when thinking or reading, which creates muscular tension and interferes with *deep psychophysiological relaxation*. Can be detected and corrected by use of the *electromyograph*.

Sufism. A system of belief that originated as a mystical sect of Islam, but is more generally used to mean "the inner secret teaching that is contained within every religion" (Idries Shah). The Sufis' "teaching stories" elicit the intuitive mode of knowing of the *right hemisphere* as a way of showing that increased knowledge without a corresponding change in being is worthless.

Superconsciousness. The union of the individual consciousness with the group unconscious with full cognitive control. See *Enlightenment*.

Syndrome. A complex coming together of the various symptoms of a disease.

Sympathetic nervous system. That part of the *autonomic nervous system*, opposite to the *parasympathetic nervous system*, invoked by the *fight-or-flight response*, which acts by secreting specific hormones to bring about the physiological changes of increased blood pressure, heart rate and body metabolism.

Syntaxtic. Gowan's term for a mode of knowing which depends on an agreed system of signs such as a public language. This dependence, which is dependence on the *left hemisphere*, inhibits other ways of knowing through symbolism by the *right hemisphere*. See teaching stories of *Sufism*.

Tanden. See *Saiketanden*.

Theta. The electrical activity of the brain changing within the range of four to seven times per second.

Transcendent function. Jung's term for both the process and the method which facilitates the transition from one psychic condition to another by means of the mutual confrontation of opposites. The terms of the conflict are integrated at a new level of synthesis.

Transcendental Meditation. A form of Mantram Yoga introduced to the West by Maharishi Mahesh Yogi, in which the person is given a specific personal mantra, or sound, on which to meditate as a means of focusing attention.

Transpersonal psychology. The title given to an emerging force in psychology which is concerned with the empirical study of the needs and values inherent in man, considered primarily as a spiritual being. See *Self-actualization, Psychosynthesis*.

Trophotrophic response. The *relaxation response*, which is the very opposite of stress (the *fight-or-flight response*).

Tumo. The Yogis' term for the power to regulate bodily heat voluntarily.

Voluntary control of internal states (VCIS). An *altered state of consciousness* in which the individual can regulate levels of nervous arousal, muscle tension, alpha and theta states, body temperature and so on, through *passive volition* in the self-conscious waking state.

Yoga. A mystic discipline directed to attaining a union (yoga) of the personal and impersonal self (individual consciousness and group unconscious) through the inhibition of the modifications of the mind, in meditation, concentration and contemplation.

Zen Buddhism. A system of belief supposed to have originated in an incident in which the Buddha, in response to a request for teaching, held up a flower in silence. Hence the claim for modern Zen to have no reliance upon teaching or upon words. It is essentially an experience. Consequently, the character of Zen does not lend itself to definition beyond a refusal of attachment to things, people, ideas, existence. Asked, "What is Zen?" the Zen teacher, Ummon, replied, "That's it." See *Soto Zen* and *Rinzai Zen*.

Zazen. A technique of Zen meditation in which the exhalations and inhalations of the breath are counted in cycles of one to ten.

Appendix E

Glossary of Sanskrit Words Used in this Book

Ajapa. Involuntary repetition; especially in reference to the sound made in breathing which is uttered fifteen times each minute.

Ajna. A *chakra* (q.v.) or vital center for certain functions, which is situated in the center of the head at the level of the eyebrows.

Ajjava. Honesty, integrity.

Akasha. Ether. One of the material elements.

Anahata. A *chakra* or vital center for certain functions, situated at the level of the heart.

Arahant. One who is free from all defilements and impurities through the realization of Nirvana, and who is free from rebirth.

Arjuna. Disciple of Krishna, to whom the *Gita* was recited.

Asana. Seat; particular posture or way of sitting.

Atman or atma. The Real Self, beyond mind and body.

Avatar. A divine incarnation, such as Krishna or Buddha.

Avidya. Ignorance, the worst of the five hindrances to progress.

Bhakti. Worship, religious devotion, devotion as service.

Bhavana. Meditation, mental culture, the dwelling of the attention on some object or idea.

Bija. A seed. Refers especially to a kind of mantra.

Bhikkus. Buddhist monks, mendicant monks.

Bodhi. Supreme knowledge.

Brahma or Brahman. The utterly divine spirit or God.

Buddhi. The higher intelligence, concerned with wisdom, not mere knowledge.

Chakra. A wheel or vital center in the spinal cord, governing certain functions.

Chitrini. An exceedingly fine canal stated to exist within the spinal cord.

Chitta. The ordinary, more or less automatically functioning mind.

Deva. A divine being or god.

Devi. A goddess.

Dharma. The law, duty, proper way of life.

Dharana. Concentration, exclusive attention to one object or idea for an extended time.

Dhyana. Meditation, state of higher consciousness, undeviating attention to one object or idea.

Gautama Buddha. The founder of Buddhism.

Gayatri. A famous mantra.

Granthi. A knot or point in the *chitrini* where there is an obstruction to the passage of Kundalini.

Guru. A spiritual teacher (the word means "weighty").

Hatha yoga. A school of Yoga concerned mainly with bodily practices.

Karma. Action and appropriate result not limited by time or space; may apply to groups, i.e., families, countries.

Karma Yoga. Actions carried out selflessly for the benefit of others.

Krishna. The divine incarnation who spoke the *Gita*.

Kundalini. Vital force or power which resides near the base of the spine.

Laya Yoga. The attainment of union with the divine through the power of Kundalini.

Mahadeva. The great god, Shiva.

Mantra. A word or sentence of power.

Mandala. A magic circle or design; religious symbol of wholeness.

Maya. Illusion.

Muladhara. The basal *chakra* at the bottom of the spine.

Nirvana. The extinction of all desires.

Padma. A lotus; another name for a *chakra*.

Padmasana. The lotus posture.

Patanjali. The author of *Aphorisms of Yoga* (the Yoga Sutras), believed to have lived about 200 B.C.

Prana. Breath; the first of the five vital airs.

Raja Yoga. Royal Yoga, the yoga of mind mastery.

Sahasrara. The thousand-petaled lotus at the crown of the head.

Samadhi. Contemplation; higher meditation; superconsciousness.

Sanskaras. Psychic knots, stresses in the nervous system which are the results of experiences and which influence future thoughts and actions.

Siddhi. One of the eight occult powers attained through meditation.

Tantras. Certain scriptures forming a set of very detailed rules for meditation, worship and the attainment of *siddhis*.

Trikona. A triangle.

Upanishads. Philosophical sections of the ancient scriptures of India.

Vedas. The ancient scriptures of India.

Yoga. Union; science of uniting the individual mind with the Universal Spirit.

Zazen. Sitting in Zen; Zen meditation (Japanese).

Zen. An attitude toward life and religion, characterized by "direct pointing," originating from the Buddha and developed in Japan. "Zen" (Japanese) is derived from the Sanskrit *dhyana*.

Index

ABOUT THE AUTHORS

C. MAXWELL CADE studied medicine and clinical psychology at London University before joining the RAFVR as an air-crew cadet in World War II. He was awarded the Royal Aeronautical Society's Navigation Prize in 1958 for a paper on Radioastronavigation. He carried out twenty-five years' research on radiation physics, both in the Royal Naval Scientific Service and in industry, and was for ten years Medical Physics Manager of a large international company. He twice won (1959 and 1960) the Radio Industry Council Award for Technical Writing, with papers on infrared physics. For several years, he was a Member of Council, and from 1973 to 1975 was Honorary Secretary of the Society for Psychical Research. He has twice been awarded the Oliver Lodge Research Grant of the College of Psychic Studies (1975/76 and 1976/77).

For the past eight years (the first three with Dr. Ann Woolley-Hart, a physician), he has been engaged in research into biofeedback and mind-body correlates of altered states of consciousness. He is a fellow of the Institute of Electrical Engineers, a member of the Institute of Physics, a member of the Institute of Biology, a fellow of the Royal Society of Health, a fellow of the Royal Society of Medicine and an Honorary Member of the National Council of Psychotherapists.

NONA COXHEAD has written six novels, two biographies and numerous articles and short stories. Her most recent nonfiction work is *Mindpower, The Emerging Pattern of Current Research*, published by Heinemann and Penguin in the United Kingdom and St. Martin's Press in the United States.